John Moore Capes

The Mosaic-worker's daughter

Vol. III

John Moore Capes

The Mosaic-worker's daughter
Vol. III

ISBN/EAN: 9783337040864

Printed in Europe, USA, Canada, Australia, Japan

Cover: Foto ©ninafisch / pixelio.de

More available books at **www.hansebooks.com**

THE

MOSAIC-WORKER'S DAUGHTER.

A NOVEL.

BY

J. M. CAPES.

IN THREE VOLUMES.
VOL. III.

LONDON:
RICHARD BENTLEY, NEW BURLINGTON STREET.
1868.

CONTENTS OF VOL. III.

CHAPTER		PAGE
I.	IN THE HOUSE OF THE TRAGIC POET	1
II.	THE MISERIES OF THE CONFESSIONAL	24
III.	LISTENING IN THE TWILIGHT	57
IV.	NOEL AND HELEN	74
V.	NOEL IN HIS DESPAIR	94
VI.	THE SACRISTAN AT HOME	110
VII.	ON THE ROAD TO PÆSTUM	132
VIII.	D'URBINO'S EYES ARE OPENED	166
IX.	GEORGIONE'S RETURN HOME	189
X.	THE INVESTIGATION	211
XI.	BIANCA GABRIELLI	237
XII.	FOR THE WEARY, REST	258

THE

MOSAIC-WORKER'S DAUGHTER.

CHAPTER I.

IN THE HOUSE OF THE TRAGIC POET.

WHILE it was being agreed between D'Urbino and Francesca, that nothing should be said about the proceedings of Donato, until the Sandfords should return to Rome, a similar course was resolved on by the travellers themselves, though for very different reasons. The Marchese could not endure the idea that the fair name of a young lady whom he hoped to marry should be sullied, as he thought it would be, by being brought before the public in connection with so strange a story. Determined as he was to prosecute his suit, he still condemned the exploit of the two cousins as a most unfeminine escapade; and found his only consolation in reflecting that not Helen, but Margaret, had been the leader in the adventure.

As to Evelyn, he kept his own counsel from mixed motives. He was honestly anxious to do nothing that should compromise Francesca, and he entertained no real doubt that the scoundrel's insinuations about her were a false fabrication. But at the same time, he was specially anxious that Mrs. Sandford should take no fresh alarm, or imagine that her house was in danger of midnight intrusions from the criminal population of Rome. Houses to suit her wishes were becoming extremely scarce, and if she were once driven from her present home by any absurd fears, she would in all probability leave Rome altogether; a proceeding that would be singularly distasteful to him, now that he was beginning to suspect that he was no longer indifferent to the fair Margaret.

Thus it was that no communication passed between himself and the remainder of the party. The weather, too, was so fine as to tempt them to all such out-of-door excursions as they could think of to while away the time. Margaret had rapidly recovered her health and spirits, and Helen spent hours every day in watching the process of what is called " coming to a mutual understanding " between the almost avowed lovers. What puzzled her was the demeanour of the ever courteous and respectful Della Porta.

He was, in truth, the very model of a young nobleman, of the essentially modern Roman type. A trifle above the average height, sufficiently good-looking, without being positively handsome; carefully dressed, almost up to the point of dandyism ; a vast deal too self-conscious ; highly respectable in his whole conduct, and perfectly well aware that he was so; he at the same time possessed a latent fund of good sense, which asserted itself whenever his healthier impulses broke through the conventionalities of thought and demeanour which he had prescribed to himself.

"I like the man," Helen would say to herself, "and yet he fidgets and annoys me; but what he is after is more than I can comprehend. To me he is horribly civil and deferential, and were he not incapable of anything so ill-bred and abominable, I should often think that he was making game of me with his absurd concurrence in everything I happen to propose. And what can possibly induce him to fancy that he is beginning to succeed with Margaret? Whenever she appears he positively brightens up, as if he were quite relieved from the necessity of showing attention to my heavy and stupid self. Well! the sooner he is out of his misery, the better for the poor man; and when he does pluck up courage

to take me into his confidence, it will only
be merciful to tell him that he has not a
chance of success."

Such especially were Helen's meditations
on the Marchese on the morning of a day
which had been fixed upon for an excursion
to Pompeii. Evelyn, who hated crowds,
now that he was wholly engrossed with his
love-making, had ascertained that nothing
special would be going on, and that the
lately renewed excavations were again suspended. The Marchese was excited, almost
up to the stage of positive vivacity; and
the ladies were in an appropriately sympathetic condition of cheerfulness and animation. As the open carriage which was to
convey them would not contain the whole
party withinside, it had been agreed between the Marchese and Evelyn that the
latter should mount the box on the way to
Pompeii, and that the former should take
the same place on the return.

Neapolitan hired horses are not often the

most spirited of quadrupeds, and therefore when Evelyn took the reins out of the driver's hands, to beguile the tedium of his half solitary position, he expected but little pleasure or excitement from the amusement of guiding the pair of bays through the streets of Naples. The streets were, however, so thronged, that it tasked his skill to the utmost to steer the hard-mouthed brutes through the crowd of carts, carriages, and waggons which filled the thoroughfares along which their route lay. The animals proved, moreover, not quite the sluggish creatures that he expected, and the drive promised to be a far more exciting affair than he had thought possible.

All went smoothly, nevertheless, until they were well out of the city streets, and were trotting rapidly along a comparatively unfrequented suburb, when taking the opportunity to turn round and address a word or two to the ladies behind, Evelyn perceived one of those extraordinary two-wheeled carriages in which the Neapolitan multitude delights to take its pleasure, gaining rapidly upon him. Perched upon its scarlet seats were some half-dozen men and women, among whom a brown-cloaked Capuchin friar, a half-clad Lazzarone, a brightly-dressed countrywoman, and a young girl were the most prominent personages. The driver was clinging to a narrow board in front of the whole, clasping one of the shafts with his twisted legs, and vainly striving to hold in the vicious brute that was galloping on at an alarming pace.

Evelyn taking in the true state of the case at a glance, shouted to the man to pull hard and to hold his tongue, instead of frightening the horse still more with his idiotic cries; while the unemployed driver by his own side, gesticulated to the same effect with all the frantic energy of his race. It was all in vain, however; the huge gig gained upon the Sandford carriage faster and faster, and as it dashed up by its side,

Evelyn's whole strength was required to hold in his own horses, excited as they were by the presence of the unmanageable beast that was distancing them, and by the voices of the men and women screaming aloud in their terrors.

As the gig began to go a-head the full danger of the situation appeared. It swerved to and fro as its driver became less and less able to control himself, and therefore made matters worse instead of better by his passionate dragging at the reins which he still contrived to hold. At every fresh swerve it seemed as if the ill-made machine must come with a crash to the ground. Happily at this moment Evelyn and the driver by his side were able to force their own horses into a slightly slackened speed, when to the infinite surprise and alarm of Mrs. Sandford and the two cousins, Della Porta quietly placed himself upon the step of the carriage, preparing to let himself down upon the road.

Noticing the movement, and knowing its extreme danger, Evelyn, who chanced to look round, called aloud to the Marchese to take heed to what he was doing, expecting to see him dashed headlong upon the ground the moment his hands parted from the handle of the carriage door to which he held. Della Porta, however, knew well what he was doing, and still clinging to the door handle, he supported himself for an instant or two while the carriage half dragged him along, until he was in the full swing of a rapid run himself.

Once safely on foot he started forwards at a rate of which every one present had imagined him to be totally incapable, and at once gained upon the terrified brute in the gig, whose onward speed was lessened by every lurch it made from one side to the other of the road. Dashing up to its head, he seized the bridle, and though powerless to force the big-boned animal to a standstill, he succeeded in so far moderating its speed as to allow him to run without much difficulty by its side, till some frightened foot-passengers who watched its course in helpless stupidity could come forward to his aid.

The steaming, panting, and trembling horse then at last gave in, and escaping from the torrent of inarticulate thanks of the persons he had saved from frightful injuries and possible deaths, the Marchese waited till Evelyn brought up the Sandford carriage, now advancing at a foot's pace. Evelyn's face was radiant with pleasure as he congratulated the Marchese on the success of his plucky exploit, and he laid his hand upon his shoulder as he stepped up into the carriage, uttering only an expressive " Bravo !" which went straight to the heart of the gratified Italian. Neither Mrs. Sandford nor the cousins could speak, from the fulness of their agitation, but as they one after another shook hands with him, he understood all that could have been said by the most eloquent of words.

By the time that Pompeii was reached a somewhat subdued manner in the three ladies and an unusually cheerful and gratified look upon the Marchese's countenance, were the only remaining signs of an adventure that might have ended in an appalling catastrophe, and they entered the wonderful ruins, prepared to yield themselves to the enjoyment of the thoughts which it awakes in all but the most dull or ignorant of common-place sight-seers. Five is at all times a somewhat awkward number in expeditions where a sympathetic companionship is a necessary condition of unhampered pleasures, and in the present party its awkwardness was soon felt. Della Porta's sole wish was to appropriate Helen to himself, while Evelyn cared only to pair off with her cousin. But what was to be done with Mrs. Sandford? Well aware that she would be *de trop*, so far as the Marchese was concerned, she was on the point of attaching herself to her niece and Evelyn, in whose conversation she had never detected anything beyond the gossip of old friends.

For a time the teasing attentions of the professed "guide," who insisted on exercising his right to instruct and worry such strangers as submitted to the torture, kept the five visitors together, while Evelyn and Della Porta were privately discussing the possibility of getting rid of the man's presence by giving him a needlessly large fee and politely dismissing him. Fortunately for their purses a deliverer, in the person of Henry Noel, made his appearance, just as they were about to enter the " House of the tragic poet," as it is called, and the irrepressible Cicerone was on the point of beginning his stereotyped discourse on the tesselated terrier and the accompanying "*cave canem*" at the door-way.

"At last we have found you, Mr. Noel," exclaimed Helen, "and now your first duty is to dismiss this abominable guide, and your second is to give an account of yourself, and tell us why you have not been near us since we came to Naples."

"The first duty is easily accomplished," he replied, exhibiting no signs of gratification at the unlooked for meeting. "As to the second, I am much occupied, and indeed it is duty that brings me here to-day. But," he added, after returning the greeting with which he was met, "if Mrs. Sandford will allow me, I shall be happy to show her all the things best worth seeing, and so set every one at liberty."

It was a crafty device of Noel's to make this offer, his sole wish being to escape from the presence of Helen; but it pleased everybody, little as he contemplated the agreeable result. Della Porta instantly decided that the golden opportunity was come, and a very small amount of ingenious manœuvring was all that was necessary to separate himself and Helen from their companions. These two latter were just leaving the famous home where the poet is supposed to have lived, and after a few rather incoherent remarks upon the traces of the paintings that were yet to be found unremoved and undestroyed, the Marchese made some excuse for inducing Helen to sit down upon a fragment of marble, and seated himself at what he thought was a correct distance before her. His manner altogether convinced her that the expected confidential communication was now to be made, and pitying him for his inevitable disappointment, she began the conversation herself.

"You must indeed be tired, Marchese," she said; "but we are rejoiced to find that you have come out of that exploit without serious injury"

"I am not in the least hurt, thank you," he replied, delighted at the expression of her sympathy.

"And I am very glad to have a moment or two with you," she continued, " in order to say how much we all admired your self sacrifice and courage in flying to the help of those unfortunate people."

The poor Marchese's heart bounded with joy.

"I think I would have done it, even if there had been no one here to encourage me," he rejoined. "As it was, in such a presence, I had not time to think of fear."

"It is coming on," thought Helen, with difficulty repressing an inclination to smile. What she said was on quite another subject.

"This is a wonderfully interesting place," she observed; "but either the Pompeians lived a most uncomfortable existence, or their sensibility to cold must have been very much less than that of modern Italians."

"Yet there was the same sensibility to the hopes and fears and passions of the heart as there is among us all to this day," he replied.

"Yes?" said Helen to herself, "it is certainly coming," adding, aloud, "I wonder whether in those days they took disappointments more easily than we do now."

He did not like the mention of disappointments at all, and resolved to make the plunge without more ado.

"I am afraid I should not bear disappointments very well myself," he said; "at least one disappointment in particular would wound me very deeply. Miss Sandford," he continued, "we do not know very much of each other, but I am sure you are an extremely kind-hearted woman."

"Not so much as you imagine, Marchese," returned Helen; "but I should like to know that you are a man who can take the disappointments of life without being too much cast down."

"Good heavens!" said the troubled Della Porta to himself; "is this the way that English girls refuse a man before he has declared himself?"

By way of reply to her strange words, he only said that he had never encountered any heavy trial, and he was afraid he should bear such things very ill.

"You are young, too," Helen went on, "and young men's hearts are not easily broken."

The bewildered man was at his wits' end.

"That depends upon the heaviness of the blow with which they are struck," he replied, with an intensity of sadness which moved Helen's commiseration for him.

"It will be a poor consolation to you, I fear," Helen continued; "but still I must now add that we feel for you all the more because of the high respect in which we shall always hold you, after your heroic conduct this morning."

"You say *we*, Miss Sandford," he replied, no longer attempting to mask his bewilderment. "Do I understand that Miss Osborne is aware of my sentiments as well as yourself."

"I am not certain as to that," said Helen, with inexplicable candour; "but considering her long intimacy with me, I have been a little surprised that she has never spoken to me on the subject. But after all, it may be only a fancy of mine, and I was wrong to hint it to any one. What I regret the most is that you should have declared yourself so seriously, as the result must cause you so much unnecessary pain. Indeed, I have been often astonished that you were not long ago undeceived."

The Marchese here rose from his seat, and looked first at Helen, then on the ground, then at Helen again, and then on the ground once more.

"Suppose we examine one or two more of these ruined homes," Helen suggested, thinking to divert the poor man's thoughts, "and then we will rest again."

So saying, she led the way out; he followed her without replying, and tried vainly to listen to the talk with which she sought to beguile him from his woes, as they wandered from one street to another. She was about giving up the task in despair, when she caught a glimpse of a sight which sent a flush of pleasure upon her cheeks, and brightened still more her always brilliant eyes. Margaret and Evelyn were slowly approaching the spot where she and Della Porta were standing, Margaret's arm linked in Evelyn's, and every movement and gesture announcing the happy termination of their anxieties.

They were close upon Helen before Margaret lifted her eyes, and the recognition was followed by an instant unlinking of her arm from that of her lover. If anything had been wanting to confirm the conclusion to which Helen had come it was this startled gesture. As they passed by, Margaret saw her cousin's smile of congratulation, and her happy look repeated the welcome tale. Then all her thoughts reverted to Della Porta, and she turned to him with the intention of breaking to him the new relation in which her cousin and her friend now stood to one another.

" I cannot tell you, Marchese," she began,

"how grieved I am for you. But you saw them pass by just now, and surely you must see that you have no hope."

"Miss Sandford," rejoined Della Porta, "my head must surely be affected by my anxieties. What is it that you are saying to me? Why should I be grieved if, as I have long suspected, the old friendship of Mr. Evelyn and Miss Osborne is ripening into something more?"

"Then you don't care so very much for her after all," cried Helen; "and I have been wasting my pity upon a mere piece of sentimentalism."

"I care for Miss Osborne much, as a cultivated and well-bred acquaintance," he answered, "but is it possible that you have thought that I regarded her in any other light?"

"Then what is it that you *do* mean?" she asked, gazing at him full in the face.

"I mean, Miss Sandford," replied Della Porta, looking downwards with a singular and sincere humility of manner, "that I have had the presumption to allow my feelings to attach themselves to yourself."

Helen sank amazed upon a seat close by, and clasped her hands together in despair.

"Oh! why," she cried, "did I not know this before? It has been a cruel deception indeed!"

The Marchese saw without the possibility of mistake that Mrs. Sandford's prediction was correct, and he received his first lesson in the ways of a woman's heart. By a happy inspiration he resolved to say nothing more, until Helen should have recovered herself enough to speak again of her own accord. His patience was sorely tried, for Helen's sole proceeding was to press her hands upon her eyes, as if to repress by force the agitation of the brain within. Once or twice he was on the verge of addressing her, but refrained. At last she spoke to him.

"This is worse than the other mistake," she said, with a calmness that he thought terrible.

"Do you give me no hope?" he replied, venturing gently to take her hand.

She withdrew it, but without irritation. Clearly he had not offended her, but she said, "I can give you none."

Again they remained silent for the time. Then it was he who began.

"Then I will wait," he said, in a voice only just audible to her.

"It is useless," she murmured.

"But I will wait, nevertheless," he replied.

"It is useless, indeed," she repeated.

"Yet the prize is worth waiting for," he answered.

"You will not think so, if we happen to meet often after we go back to Rome," replied Helen. "At any rate, Marchese," she added, in a livelier tone, "we shall always wish each other well. And here are the others come searching after their lost companions. Mamma," she added, going up to her mother, " I think we have all had enough of Pompeii for to-day."

CHAPTER II.

THE MISERIES OF THE CONFESSIONAL.

DISTRESSED and agitated as Henry Noel had been when he first learnt that the very woman from whose presence he was flying had followed him to the very city in which he sought the distraction by which he hoped to quiet the throbbing of his still unconquered passion, he could not so far neglect the work he had undertaken as to leave Naples at once. He rested his chief expectations of comparative tranquillity upon the nature of his occupation, which would keep him employed in the very last district of the city into which English visitors would be likely to penetrate. His chance encounter with the Sandford party at Pompeii made him resolve to avoid every spot to which the love of sight-seeing might tempt them, and inasmuch as nearly the whole of his time would be spent within the obscurest churches of Naples, he regarded himself as practically secure from all danger.

Just now, too, he happened to be charged with an additional duty which would confine him more or less to a part of the city totally unfrequented by strangers. The parish priest of *San Pietro della Croce* had been obliged to leave his post for a few days through illness, and as Noel would necessarily be spending some hours daily in the church or its neighbourhood, he had asked Noel, who was prepared with the needful episcopal permission, to hear the confessions of any of his parishioners who might be in such haste to unburden their consciences as to be unwilling to wait for their regular pastor's return. It was most improbable, he said, that any such application would be made, but as Noel would be on the spot, he would perhaps take his place for the occasion if called for. To this Noel agreed, and the parish priest went his way satisfied.

The parish, as it happened, was one of the worst in the whole of Naples, being little better than a nest of tall houses built in extremely narrow streets, or rather lanes, and inhabited by a population one-half of which was reputed to be connected, either by blood or interest, with some of the most notorious of the brigands who still infected the more distant country districts, and who at times attacked travellers in the neighbourhood of Naples itself. They were, in truth, such an ill-looking race of scoundrels, that Noel, who was a thoroughly courageous man, would scarcely have liked to be seen much among them, were it not that he was assured that their superstitious veneration for every member of the priesthood was as profound as was their disregard for all laws, divine and human.

On the day after the departure of the parish priest, on entering the church in the course of the morning, his attention was drawn to a kneeling figure in front of an image of the Madonna, placed over an altar in a small chapel on one of the sides of the nave. The image was dressed up in the usual trumpery tawdry finery so popular with the Neapolitan populace, and all round it were hanging those strange votive offerings by which the Italian poor are wont to express their gratitude for favours granted, as they imagine, to the intercession of their favourite saints.

It was notorious that some of these offerings were brought by the brutal highwaymen themselves, and were an expression of thankfulness for success in crime. Incomprehensible as it seems to those who are not familiar with the forms which superstition takes among the Italian poor, it is undeniable that many a brigand will implore the help of the Madonna or some other popular saint in the violence which he is plotting against his innocent victim, and will hold himself bound by the heaviest penalties to present the offerings which he promises, as a sort of bribe, to the objects of his veneration.

Nor are the absurdity and the wickedness of the practice so manifest to the ignorant mind as we are apt to suppose. Crimes of robbery, violence and murder, are practically judged in the Italian brigand classes by a standard of their own. Even if they do not go so far as to hold it a perfectly right and Christian thing to get their livings at the expense of the property and lives of other people, they certainly view the system of brigandage as a species of necessary evil, and its sins, if sins they are, as being so essentially venial in their nature, that they can be almost sanctified by previous petitions to the Virgin Mary, or any other canonised personage, provided only that the vows then made in hopes of success are duly fulfilled when the contemplated crimes have been happily accomplished.

How far the parish priest of *San Pietro della Croce* was cognisant of the scandalous origin of some of the waxen representations before which the strange-looking man was praying, was not known to Noel, who, in truth, abstained from asking awkward questions, with as much caution as if he had been born an Italian. Nevertheless, he felt convinced that the devout-looking stranger was one of the very class whose prayers were in reality an apparatus for quieting the inconvenient scruples of a conscience not yet absolutely hardened in guilt. After watching him for a brief space, however, he passed on into the sacristy to begin the work on which he was engaged

In the sacristy he found Tolomeo, the old sacristan of the church, looking fidgety and uncomfortable ; and though he had no particular liking for the man, he could not refrain from asking him if he knew anything of the apparently devout suppliant in the small chapel. Tolomeo was, in fact, hovering about in the hope of having this very question put to him.

"It is Lorenzo Galli," he replied. "Your reverence knows who Lorenzo Galli is."

"I never heard of him in my life, Tolomeo," replied Noel.

"Is it possible?" exclaimed the sacristan, with an amazed look. "But walls have ears, *stimatissimo Padre*, and it is safest to say nothing, though it is reported that Lorenzo is now converted and going to become a man of peace."

And with that he abruptly left Noel, and went from the sacristy into the church. Presently he returned, and mysteriously beckoned to Noel to follow him. Wondering what could be going on, Noel obeyed, and walked behind Tolomeo till they reached a place where the kneeling figure was visible. The man was still on the same spot as before, but was prostrate on his face upon the stone floor. Every now and then he partially raised his head, and then fell forwards, again, actually striking the stones with his forehead. At length, he rose so far as to remain upright upon his knees, and beat his breast with violence, and Noel could distinctly he r the rapid tones in which he poured forth the Paternosters and Ave Marias of the Rosary.

"He will be a Saint!" whispered Tolomeo in Noel's ear, with scarcely suppressed exultation. "And they say he has killed more than a dozen men in his day. And as to robberies and mutilations, God only knows how many."

Presently the man's devotions became more quiet, and Noel betook himself to the sacristy. He had not long recommenced his work, when Tolomeo again appeared, looking as radiant with pleasure as so ugly a little old man could possibly look.

"Your reverence is wanted immediately," he replied to Noel's remonstrance against the interruption. " He wants to confess immediately. Praise be to God, and his holy mother, for the same !"

" Who wants to confess ?" asked Noel, in dismay, by no means gratified with the prospect of confessing and absolving a penitent brigand, with a dozen murders upon his conscience.

" Lorenzo, your reverence," returned the sacristan. " Oh ! what ' a blessing for you."

" Would it not be better for him to wait till the priest of the parish returns, Tolomeo ?" Noel timidly asked.

" Impossible ! father," rejoined the sacristan, wondering that the young English ecclesiastic was not eager for the duty. " He knows that you are here, for he questioned me before you came, and he is in torrents of tears, and says that it is impossible to wait."

Noel felt that there was nothing for it but to submit; but he put forward the plea that he had only an imperfect acquaintance with the Neapolitan patois.

"*Gesu! Maria! Giuseppe!*" exclaimed the excited Tolomeo; "God will help your reverence to understand him. Besides, Lorenzo, poor fellow, is not an ignorant countryman, but was a student for the priesthood before he was punished by a cruel judge for a trifle of stabbing, and was obliged to take to the mountains for his living, poor man."

With a sigh that but faintly expressed his annoyance, Noel then proceeded to seat himself in a confessional in the church, to which Tolomeo immediately conducted the agitated Galli, with the information that the *Padre forestiere* was a *galant'uomo*, though, he supposed, a little rigorist in his view of things. Uttering the appointed form for commencing the confidential communication, Noel waited for the man to begin his statement. For some time nothing but sighs and sobbing could be heard through the small grating to which Noel's ear was applied, for the purpose of hearing what was to be said by the penitent kneeling on the other side of the partition which separated him from the confessor. Noel therefore spoke a few words of encouragement, which soon quieted the man's excitement so far as to allow him to begin his story.

It was, in substance, and apart from the interminable ejaculations of self-reproach with which it was intermingled, a statement that he had been persuaded by a country girl with whom he had fallen in love, to renounce his brigand life, and as a preliminary to their marriage, to make his peace with the church, by a full confession of his sins. Noel at first thought this a somewhat unsatisfactory explanation of the vehemence of the man's apparent penitence, but recollecting the impulsiveness of the Neapolitan nature, he took it for granted that having honestly undertaken to reform himself, though only to please the girl he wished to marry, the long-smothered early feelings of the brigand's youth had asserted themselves as soon as he came within the influence of religious observances.

He soon satisfied himself that it was really to this cause that the man's excited emotions were due, for he found that the heart of the ex-brigand was still with his late companions, and that he was very unwilling to confess any of his enormities in such a definite manner as to allow a confessor to judge of their real character. Though Noel had been some years a priest, he had not been in the habit of receiving the confessions of many people, and had never fallen into the prevalent lax interpretation of the system laid down by Roman casuists, for the guidance of confessors in dealing with their penitents. Thinking it, therefore, his duty to insist upon something more distinct than the mystifying generalities with which the half-converted Galli wished to satisfy him, he proceeded to probe the man's conscience with such a series of questions as he thought best calculated to extract the truth from him in all its native hideousness.

And a frightful tale it was, so far as the wretched man could be brought to enter into the details which betrayed the full enormity of his crimes. As he admitted one cold-blooded atrocity after another, still unwilling to look upon them with any real horror or sorrow, Noel's heart felt sick within him, and he began to doubt whether he should have strength or courage to proceed. All at once his attention was roused to a still more painful intensity. The man stated that quite recently he had been one of a party who had attacked the carriage of some Italian travellers journeying from Naples into the interior of the country. Only one man had been killed, and he was the postilion; and Galli actually put forward an excuse for the act as a perfectly harmless accident, on the ground that if he and his comrades had not wasted their time in robbing these Italians, who had but little money in their purses, they would have attacked a large party of English ladies and gentlemen, who would have resisted, and there would have been a great deal of blood-shedding. He added that they might have carried off the ladies into the mountains, and that his old comrades would still succeed in so doing before the following week was past.

Remembering that there were not very many English families in Naples at the time, a horrible thought crossed Noel's mind. Was it possible that it could be the Sandfords and their friends who had escaped this hideous danger, a danger, too, which might be still hanging over their heads? Yet if he showed any sign of an anxiety to learn more about the persons thus cursorily referred to, Galli might take alarm and refuse to give him any further information.

After pausing to take breath, and to collect his thoughts, he ventured upon a question which he imagined would rouse no suspicion.

"Then you think it no crime to kill an Italian," he said—the whole dialogue being, of course, conducted in the lowest possible tones of voice—" or at any rate a less crime to kill Italian than English people."

"Bah! *padre mio*," replied Galli, " it is of less account to kill a Neapolitan than an Englishman, because those devils of English bring the soldiers and the government down upon us."

" But how do you know that these persons who escaped you were really English?" asked Noel.

" I have seen them, *mio padre*," said Galli, who had not the remotest suspicion that Noel was an Englishman, having taken him all along for a Roman.

" But you may be mistaken, nevertheless," Noel suggested.

"I have seen English before," said Galli, "and I saw these ladies in the balcony of their house."

"And did you expect them to carry a

large sum of money with them?" asked Noel.

"Their ransom would have been ten thousand, twenty thousand, thirty thousand, *colonnati, mio padre,* if we had carried them to the mountains. The water-carrier who supplies them is my friend, and says that Miladi Sandford is as rich as a princess."

The cold drops of water broke out in streams upon the head of the miserable Noel, as the dreaded name fell from the ex-brigand's lips; but he had sufficient control over himself to say nothing further on that point at the moment, and he went back to the earlier portion of the man's confession, asking for further explanations, and putting such questions as might gradually lead them back to the peril still threatened to his English friends.

"You have not told me," he began, "how many of these murders were premeditated, and how many were the result of sudden passion."

"As to that," replied Galli, "your reverence may be aware that I am not like some others that I know of."

"What do you mean?" Noel asked.

"I never kill any man, or at least any woman," said Galli, "unless it is necessary."

"What do you mean," asked Noel, "by speaking of a horrible crime as necessary?"

"It is necessary, *mio padre*," said the man, "when persons are so foolish as to resist. Then their blood is upon their own heads."

"Then you admit that you always attack travellers with the intention of murdering them if they resist," Noel replied. "You intend to commit murder in every case, if it is convenient to you."

"What would you have, Eccellenza?" said Galli, "it is necessary for us to succeed; and if men are fools enough not to submit, it is not our fault if we sometimes kill them."

All Noel's belief in the sincerity of the man's repentance vanished at this reply. He saw that the moment he was brought to face his crimes one by one, and seen in their true colours, all his newly aroused emotions yielded to the habitual sophistry of a hardened criminal. At the same time, the perception of this fact made it all the more important that he should employ the utmost care in dealing with a man who was prepared at any moment to turn round and justify every one of his enormities.

"You say you are a better man than some of your comrades," he continued. "How can you prove that to me?"

"Your reverence must be aware," said Galli, "that we brigands sometimes have a *vendetta* against some person who has wronged us. And if we know that such a person may be one of a party which is to be plundered, we take the opportunity of killing him. That is quite natural."

"And you yourself never went on a plundering expedition, intending in this manner to gratify your private revenge. Is this what you mean?" asked Noel.

"Thanks be to God and his holy mother!" ejaculated the man, "I never cared about killing an enemy of my own."

"How was that, pray?" said Noel.

"I never had the opportunity, your reverence," Galli answered. "I never knew beforehand that any of my enemies would be in my power."

"But if you had known this," Noel suggested, "what would you have done?"

"Ah! Eccellenza," said Galli, "who can say?"

"Do you generally learn beforehand who will be the persons whom you intend to attack?" Noel asked, thinking that he had now an opening for recurring to the threatened dangers of the Sandfords.

"Sometimes, yes," said Galli, " sometimes, no."

" When you lately robbed the party of Italians and killed the postilion," Noel continued, " how long beforehand had you known anything about them ?"

" Ah ! your reverence," rejoined Galli, " that is a wonderful thing. We knew that the English ladies and their friends would be on the road, but the devil tempted us by putting these cursed Italians in our path, and so the others were gone by when we reached the wood where we were to have come upon them. But it was not my doing. Our captain has left off praying to Saint Antony, and this was the consequence."

Aware that it is the common practice with the lower class of Italians to pray to St. Antony to help them in finding their lost possessions, and generally to aid them by granting any specially desired gift, Noel was but little surprised at this fresh revelation of the degraded spiritual condition of the brigand race.*

"Then you think that if you had prayed to St. Antony to help you to find the party of English people, you would not have found them safe out of your reach;" said Noel.

"Ah! *mio padre*," said Galli, " who can say? St. Antony has always been our best friend."

"Perhaps your comrades are still hoping that he will help them to seize the same English people another day."

"Who can say?" replied Galli, unwilling to commit himself to any opinion about the future, though with no suspicion that Noel had any special object in thus questioning him. His determination to fence with every question which might possibly compromise his late companions

* The superstition of "whistling for a wind," still prevalent among English sailors, is a surviving form of the Italian belief.

was, in fact, so manifest to Noel that he soon ceased the helpless task.

And now the whole horror of the position in which he was placed began to force itself upon his thoughts. Not one word of all that he had just heard could he dare to repeat, even for the prevention of the atrocious crime which he had learnt was still in contemplation. Every syllable that the infamous villain had uttered was made sacred by the seal of sacramental confession, and he must stand by and see the perpetration of the most devilish wickedness in silent agony. He would, of course, make the attempt to induce the so-called penitent to allow him to inform the Sandfords and their friends of the diabolical scheme that was hatching against them. But the obstinate determination with which the man refused to make any communication that might injure his late comrades told Noel too plainly what would be the result of any such proposition. However, the proposition should be made, and there still remained the possibility that by refusing Galli absolution for his crimes, except on the condition of his consenting to put the English party upon their guard, he might induce him to yield. The possibility was, indeed, so faint as scarcely to exist, but such as it was, it suggested the utmost caution in acting upon it.

" You have told me," Noel resumed, " that you intend to live a reformed life."

" I do, your reverence," replied Galli.

" And you will be ready to prove your sincerity as soon as possible ?" added Noel.

" I have sworn to do it, *mio padre*," said the man, " and I never yet broke my oath."

" But supposing that I might require you to complete a painful penance as a condition of absolution," said Noel, " would you still keep to what you have sworn ?"

" What will be the penance that his reverence will impose ?" inquired Galli, his suspicions all aroused.

"Only what would be some little atonement for your past sins," Noel replied.

"A hundred paters and aves?" asked Galli.

"Not a penance of that special kind," said Noel.

"A hundred stripes?" asked the man.

"No, nothing of that kind," Noel said.

"A silver relic-box for St. Antony?" suggested Galli, in a wild effort of imagination.

"No," rejoined Noel. "The penance I shall exact will be not so very severe a one, after all; and it will be the beginning of your new life, which must for the future be devoted to the benefit of those whom you have so frightfully wronged."

"I cannot make restitution of anything," rejoined Galli, taking the alarm; "I have no money, for it was all spent as fast as it was gained."

"Suppose, then," said Noel, priding himself upon the ingenuity with which he was going to give to his proposition the aspect of a suddenly suggested alternative, "suppose that by way of a good deed you inform the English persons you mentioned of the intention of your former comrades to waylay them. There will be no harm done, and you need say nothing about your old friends' names."

"A thousand devils!" exclaimed Galli, in his astonishment at the proposition, forgetting that if he spoke above the low tone of voice always adopted in the confessional he might be heard by any chance stander by. "Does his reverence not know that we have all sworn not to betray each other?"

"Such an oath would be an unlawful oath, you must remember," Noel rejoined, in the usual murmured tone. "Being an unlawful oath, it is not binding on the conscience."

"Does not your reverence understand," continued Galli, himself again speaking low, "that on the first suspicion that I had turned traitor, I should have a dagger through my heart?"

Noel knew too well that such would in all probability be the wretched man's fate if a breath of suspicion reached his late companions in crime. He therefore suggested that there was no reason that any one should be aware from what quarter the warnings had come."

"You have only to authorise me to give the ladies a hint that they had better make no excursions from Naples," he suggested.

"Impossible!" rejoined Galli; "the secret could not be kept."

"Why is it impossible?" asked Noel.

"The plan of their excursion is all arranged, your reverence," replied the man; "and if it is broken off, suspicion will fall upon me. I am a marked man already, for they think I am going to turn traitor. I was watched when I came into the church last night; and the moment those English people change their minds, the order to stab me will be given."

"Good God!" exclaimed Noel, losing his own self-possession, "what a work of the devil it is that you are pledged to! Remember, I tell you, that if you do not step in to stop these fresh murders, the blood of others will be again upon your head, and with their blood all the guilt of the murder of the other souls that you have sent into eternity will come back upon you!"

"Why should I give my own life to save those English fools?" rejoined Galli, with a savage sulkiness that boded ill for the success of Noel's appeal. "Besides, they are safe till after Sunday next."

"You may give your life," returned Noel, with a solemn intensity that for a moment made the wretched man's heart almost stop beating with fear; "you may give your life to save these English people, but if you do not give it, what will be the eternal doom of your soul? Are you prepared for the

everlasting flames of hell? Do you not
already feel the fires closing in all around
you, scorching and burning you with never-
ending agonies? What is the momentary
stab of an assassin's knife in your heart,
compared to the piercing of the daggers
which a thousand devils will drive into you
night and day for ever? Do you not feel
it already? Do you not hear their yells of
joy with which they will strike you, and
stab you, and torture you, as you have struck
and stabbed and tortured the unhappy victims of your past crimes?"

The shiverings and shudderings of the
terror-stricken Galli, which shook the very
confessional itself, assured Noel how power-
fully his terrible words were telling upon
the crouching wretch beside him.

"Oh, God!" murmured the unhappy
man; "Oh, *Maria Santissima!* oh, father,
spare me! spare me! Is there no hope?
But I cannot die yet! I feel the knife in
my heart already! Let me live, and do

anything but this! For God's sake, father, spare me! spare me!"

"It is not for me to spare you," rejoined Noel. "It is for God to spare you, and he will not spare you if you share in the murder of these innocent persons, by refusing to give them warning of their danger. Choose which you will. Give me authority to warn them, and then fly the country, and make yourself safe from your companion's vengeance; or else live a few miserable years longer, and be damned for ever in hell!"

"Father," he rejoined, "I cannot fly. I cannot leave *her*. For her sake I have broken with my comrades; and already they are watching me, and my steps will be dogged the moment I leave this church. What are these English people to me? Why should I be murdered to save them? Let them take their chance, I say. I was a fool to come to you at all."

"Have you no mercy for the helpless women for whom this horrible fate is preparing?" said Noel, trying one more way for touching the man's hard heart.

"Mercy!" he echoed; "who ever showed me mercy? I ask you. They are no better than other women. Let them die, and be damned too, for they are only English heretics. They will only be going to hell a little before their time."

Frantic with dismay at the thought of the horrible fate which he now saw was almost certainly awaiting the woman whom he still so passionately loved, though separated from her by an impassable barrier, Noel writhed upon his seat in anguish, as he finally saw how hopeless was the task of touching the heart of the infamous villain who was still kneeling by his side in the guise of a repentant sinner. For some moments he remained speechless, and sat rocking himself backwards and forwards in his agony, his face buried in his hands, putting up a wild imploring cry to heaven to help him in his misery.

At length, still forcing himself to speak in the suppressed voice which he had hitherto necessarily employed, he leant his throbbing brow against the small grating through which the dialogue had been carried on, and once more implored the impenitent Galli to have pity upon the innocent victims whom he was sacrificing.

"As you hope for mercy when you die," he said, his panting breath scarcely allowing him to speak; "as you hope for a life of happiness now that you are to possess the one woman you love best in the world, in the name of God, and of Jesus Christ, and his mother, and all the saints, save these women who have done you no wrong."

Then straining his ear to listen for a reply to this last appeal, he waited for some signs that the guilty criminal was wavering in his resolution. No answer being returned, a faint hope rose in his mind that the man was at last moved. Still no words reached his ear, and he trembled with fear as to what was about to happen to him. The confessional was so dark that it was in vain that he looked through the grating, in order to learn what Galli was doing. When no sign was given him, and no sound was heard, he could no longer control himself, and left his seat to ascertain from without what had really taken place. A single glance showed him that the ex-brigand was gone, having stealthily moved away while Noel was in the very act of imploring him to yield to his prayers.

Still, it was possible that Galli might not have left the church, and might be intending to return and accede to Noel's entreaties. But neither in the open nave, nor in any side chapel, nor in the sacristy, was a human being to be found, the Sacristan Tolomeo having also departed; as, indeed, he was at liberty to go whenever it pleased him. Possibly, nevertheless, the man who had fled might be lingering outside, and trusting to this last hope, Noel rushed to the church-door. He turned the handle, and would have dashed through in his haste, but though the handle yielded, the door was immoveable. He was locked in alone.

CHAPTER III.

LISTENING IN THE TWILIGHT.

THE dull winter day was drawing to a close, and the gloom of the church of *San Pietro della Croce* was rapidly changing into total darkness, when the Sacristan Tolomeo returned to fulfil such duties as were necessary before closing the building for the night. Knowing that Noel would be engaged in the sacristy during the whole afternoon, he had thought it needless to come back and lock up the church for the short time during which Italian churches are for the most part closed at mid-day. Moreover, if by chance the building were left tenantless at any time, the discipline of the parish was not of so severe a kind as to make the indolent Tolomeo expect that any notice would be taken of his neglect.

He was, accordingly, a little put out of humour when he found that the key of the church door was in the lock, with its handle outside, and the door itself fastened. It seemed strange that Noel should have left the church thus unprotected, especially as he had on the previous day specially charged the sacristan to admit no person into the sacristy, while he was examining the registers and other documents which were there preserved. Being an arrant coward, like most of those Italians who are intimately connected with the Roman clergy, with whom personal courage is by no means esteemed a virtue worth cultivation, Tolomeo stepped forward into the church with some little fear, as soon as he had unlocked the door.

The dim light, which still lingered

throughout its wide space, threw the small chapels and other recesses of the building into the deepest shadow, and the feeble glimmer of the small lamp which hung in front of the high altar, increased rather than lessened the somewhat weird aspect of the silent scene. Wondering what would have become of the repenting brigand in whom he had seen the materials for a rapidly matured saint, Tolomeo cautiously came forward, turning his eyes right and left, and peering timidly into each spot where the gloom seemed most intense. At each fresh pause he muttered an *Ave Maria*, and crossed himself, before he could summon courage to proceed.

Suddenly his blood ran cold in his veins, and he trembled from head to foot. In front of one of the side altars, where the darkness was not yet complete, he descried a dark figure upon the pavement, motionless and silent as the grave. It was all but prostrate, though the half-kneeling attitude was still discernible. Whether it was man or woman, or whether it was that of a dead or a living human being, the terrified Tolomeo could not tell. He dared not approach, but stood shaking and muttering prayers, on the spot from which he had first caught sight of what he saw.

Presently a faint and long-drawn sigh assured him that whatever might be the object of his terrors, it was a living person who was before him. Still unable to face the sight which had so frightened him, Tolomeo held his breath in order that no sound should escape his ears. Before long the nearly prostrate figure raised itself so far as to convince him that it was none other than Noel himself, who then remained motionless upon his knees. Afraid to encounter him, and to receive the rebuke he expected for deserting the church during the whole of the day, Tolomeo moved backwards with noiseless steps, till he reached a totally dark recess, in which he found a seat from which he could, unobserved, watch the movements of the man whom he feared to meet.

After another long-drawn sigh, Noel began to speak aloud. Unconscious that he was no longer alone, the unhappy man gave vent to his anguish in broken phrases, sometimes in the form of prayers, sometimes in the form of bitter cries of terror and lamentation, and sometimes in the form of imprecations against the authors of all the misery which had overwhelmed him. As he spoke, Tolomeo listened with all his ears. Dread of being discovered gave place to an overpowering curiosity to hear what the man whom he feared would reveal in the fulness of his conviction that he was alone. It never occurred to him for an instant that there could be anything dishonourable or morally wrong in thus playing the eavesdropper to another person, and especially to a priest. Dishonourableness was, in truth, an idea simply unknown to Tolomeo, as it is to all such as he; and as it is, unhappily, to a large proportion of the Italian ecclesiastical body.

Here, too, was the golden opportunity so seldom given to the suspicious Neapolitan. Here was one of the very men to whom he looked up with mingled feelings of superstitious veneration and dread, about to unveil the secrets of his bosom, unconscious that any listener was near. It was a golden opportunity, indeed, and he resolved that every word that reached him should be treasured up in his memory for future meditation. Who could say, too, that he might not hear some hints as to Noel himself, which he might turn to his own good profit? A priest, he felt confident, would not give himself up to such a paroxysm of devotion and sorrow, except through the recollection of his own personal guilt. The *Padri* and *Frati* were no doubt like other men, if one could only get at the secrets of their lives; and if only they were as ready to unbosom themselves to their flocks as they were determined to keep those flocks in subjection, there would be many a tale to tell, such as the most curious had never dreamt of.

Shrinking up, therefore, still further into the darkness of the recess, and holding his breath with determined self-control, Tolomeo drank in every syllable that escaped from Noel's lip. His utterances were all in fragments, and at first the listener was bewildered as to their possible meaning. In place of the passionate confessions of crime which Tolomeo had expected, he could make out nothing except that Noel was utterly miserable, and was in bondage to some other person's wicked will.

Gradually, he pieced together a few detached words and sentences, chiefly of the nature of passionate prayers for the safety of certain persons whose names sounded strange in the sacristan's ears. They were certainly not Neapolitan names, but they might be

Roman or Tuscan, for all he could tell. Then he suddenly recollected that he had that very day learnt that Noel was not a Roman, but an Englishman; and he drew the conclusion that the persons for whom he so fervently prayed were probably English also.

All this quickened his interest in what he heard. What could be the padre's interest in these English people? By and bye Tolomeo was satisfied that the name of the brigand Lorenzo Galli occurred in a kind of vehement imprecation. Noel seemed to be addressing the man, and appealing to him to yield to some entreaty. Then it seemed as if Noel was praying for guidance as to some confession that had been made to him, in which the names of the brigand and the supposed English people were mixed up together.

Here the listener's anxiety to learn what it could all mean, proved nearly fatal to his project. He dropped his hat upon the pavement, and but for Noel's profound preoccupation, the sound would assuredly have aroused his attention. At length the sacristan was satisfied that some perils hung over the heads of the persons whose names sounded so strange in his ears, and that the very man whom he had left apparently penitent in Noel's confessional, was closely connected with it. It was in vain that he watched again for the names he had heard. They had appeared to him little better than a crowd of consonants, and though he was satisfied that he should recognise them in a moment if Noel should repeat them at another time, he could not so frame his own lips as to produce any sound sufficiently like what he had heard, to be recognised either by Noel or any other person, whether Italian or English.

With this he was forced to content himself, for Noel soon rose from his knees, and walked with weary steps in the direction of the sacristy. The moment he could do it with safety, the cunning Tolomeo then came forth from his concealment, and gained the door of the church in silence. He then immediately turned round and walked again into the church, striking the pavement with a stick which he carried, and by other similar devices suggesting the belief that he was now just entering the church. He proceeded straight to the sacristy, and uttered a well-feigned cry of surprise at finding Noel still there, and engaged in arranging his papers and books, to be deposited in a place of security for the night.

"*Gesu! Maria!*" he cried, "has his reverence not gone home yet? Does his reverence know how late it is? And could his reverence tell him who had locked the church door, and taken the key outside? And what a blessed thing it was that no thief had stolen the key! And would his reverence condescend so far as to come to his, Tolomeo's, poor lodgings, where his mother would provide him with a humble *colazione*, in case his reverence had not dined and was hungry?"

Ingenious, however, as was this device for inducing Noel to enter into a conversation, while his mind was still shaken with its late emotions, it failed entirely. Noel was in no mood for the man's intolerable chatter, and was only too glad not to enter upon the subject of the locking of the church door. With a very few words of reply, he completed the arrangements he was making, and left the discomfited Tolomeo to his solitude.

Arriving at his own lodgings, he found it impossible to shake off the horrible thoughts which were preying upon his heart. From every point of view he went over the circumstances in which he was placed, hoping to find some comfort or some peculiarity in his position which would justify him according to his own principles, in making use of the information he had received from the man Galli, for the purpose of saving Helen

Sandford and her friends. Then, again, the whole force of his nature rose up in vehement wrath against the delusion by which he had been induced to enter the priesthood, and so shut himself out from all possibility of marrying the woman whom he still so ardently loved.

"What is it to me now," he cried to himself, in the anguish of his soul, "that I was honest and sincere in the choice I made? What is it to me that they who worked upon my wretched feelings, thought that they were doing God service in binding me for life in a bondage that can never be broken? They were bound themselves in the same slavery: and they said that they were content. How am I the better for that? Now I see that it is a horrible, an accursed, a deadly, and inhuman thing, to shut me up for ever in this horrible solitude of heart, until death comes to set me free.

"Oh! Helen! Helen! oh! my love, my life, my darling! why are you torn from me? why was I so mad on that fatal day, when with my own hands I built up the wall that shut you out from me for ever? Yes! for ever! there is no hope for me until I die. My heart is broken. Oh! my God? that I could die to-day and end all my miseries!

"But what are mine to what yours, Helen, will be before many days are over? Yes! I see it all before my eyes. I see you in their accursed hands! I hear the sound of their bullets! I see the blood streaming! I hear your cries and your shrieks! I see you struggling in their devilish arms! I hear you cry for help, and there is none to come to save you! Oh God! is it possible that it is my duty to foresee all this hideous crime and agony, and not to open my lips or stir my hands to hinder it? And am I really bound to stand by and see these hellish murderers work their will upon you and all you love, when one syllable of mine would make it all impossible?"

Then came a torrent of the doubts, the fears, the hopes, and the terrors, which casuistry suggests to sensitive and conscientious minds, when torn by the conflicting passions and principles which were now raging in Henry Noel's mind. Before his wildly excited imagination, one frightful picture stood out in all its horrible brightness, and one sound kept ringing in his ears. He saw Helen striving in helpless horror in the arms of savage men, while shriek after shriek burst from her livid lips. A blurred and horrid vision of slaughtered men and women filled up the background of the maddening sight; but everything faded into indistinctness, and died away into silence, before the one figure of Helen, writhing in the blood-stained arms of her captors, and the endless screams with which she called in vain for some friend to come and save her.

At length Noel's brain, exhausted with agitation, terror and fasting, seemed to whirl round and round. A sickening sense of faintness came upon him, while he murmured, "Yes, I will save her! It can be no sin to stop this horrid crime," and he had barely strength left to totter to the nearest seat, when he sank upon it in total unconsciousness.

When gradually and slowly he recovered himself, the recollection of what he had been suffering came back in fragments of confused thought. He pressed his hand against his aching head, and struggled to realise his true position. The hideous vision of Helen and her agonising screams had almost faded from his imagination, and was succeeded by a sense, almost physical, of an iron gripe, holding him motionless in obedience to the discipline of the church, which forbade the revelation of the secrets of the Confessional, in any form or under any circumstances whatsoever. He began to feel like a martyr to his faith, voluntarily laying his head upon the block, or baring his flesh to the torturers who waited to tear it piecemeal with their horrible knives and pincers, while near at hand the ear-piercing cries of those he loved best on earth told him that the bloody torments were already at work upon their innocent limbs.

He could scarcely frame his thoughts into words, he was too much exhausted even to open his eyes; but there he sat, filled with a dull, leaden sense of suffering, past, present, and to come, and yet at heart resolved to drink the cup of agony even to the dregs. Resistance to his doom was hopeless. He could only trust that it would soon be over, for himself and others. If any one definite hope was present to his thoughts, it was the trust that Helen might die instantly and painlessly, by the first shot that the miscreants would fire. So trusting, he even began to murmur a prayer that such might be her lot; and thus praying broken sentences, such as he had been wont to read and to treasure in his memory, all taken from the narrative of the Great Tragedy enacted at Jerusalem more than eighteen centuries ago, came floating across his thoughts. Partly from utter physical and mental exhaustion, and partly from the influence of the cherished habits of his whole life, a species of helpless acquiescence stole slowly upon him, and bending his head forward upon the table before him, he fell into a heavy and dreamless sleep.

CHAPTER IV.

NOEL AND HELEN.

The evening was far advanced, when the woman who owned Noel's present lodgings, and waited upon him, wondering that she had received no summons after his return from his out-door occupations, entered the room in which he was still asleep. The noise of her entrance awoke him, and he sat up and looked full in her face, as if hardly knowing who she was, and where he found himself.

"*Gesu! Maria!*" she cried, with a sudden start, as she saw the haggardness of Noel's features, exaggerated as it was under the dim light of a single small lamp. "Your reverence is very ill!" It was in vain that he protested that he was not ill, but fatigued and weary. The woman was by no means accustomed to have her will disputed, and having no inclination or strength for resisting, it was not long before she was standing by Noel's side, compelling him to eat and drink before going to bed. With equal determination she then insisted upon his retiring at once, with the additional information that if he was not well on the following morning, she should call in a doctor, whether he approved of it or no.

When the morning came, Noel was sufficiently himself again, so far as to satisfy his landlady that the presence of the doctor was not as yet needed; but he was far too ill and too much agitated to be able to resume the work upon which he was engaged. Torn with terrible anxieties, he was still unable to satisfy himself as to the course which duty required him to pursue. He ransacked his memory for some precedent to justify himself in making use of the ex-brigand's confession, under circumstances so singular as those in which he was involved; but dreadful as was the alternative that haunted his imagination, he could recall nothing that satisfied him.

"May I not give them a hint to leave Naples immediately?" he asked himself, but the rules of the confessional say "no."

"If I hear of their making the intended excursion, may I not call upon them on the day and make some excuse for keeping them at home?"

The same inexorable laws said "no."

"May I not seek out this wretched Galli, and entreat him to spare them?"

Again the iron regulations said "no," for it would be a violation of the seal of confession even to speak to the man out of the confessional with the remotest reference to what he had confessed.

With a clear and penetrating judgment

Noel repudiated every suggestion that occurred to him for breaking the spirit, while keeping to the letter of the rule which bound him to inviolable secrecy. It is a rule, he saw as distinctly as if he had been engaged in a passionless critical discussion, without which the practice of sacramental confession must be simply impossible; and to the absolute rejection of that practice he was not even tempted for a moment. His mind was not of that character which cares for the foundations of theological creeds; as to doubting of the truth of the system in which he had been brought up, he would almost as soon have doubted of his own existence. He might rebel with frantic indignation against the mere laws and regulations of his church, and bitterly had he thus at times rebelled; but all the while his loyalty to her supreme authority, as he accounted it, was never shaken; for he was a man of action and of feeling, rather than a man of thought, and like a soldier, who has no will except to do his duty to his chief, whatever might be his personal opinions as to that chief's real aims, he was ready to die rather than doubt the claims of his church to his unwavering obedience.

In one gratification alone he considered that he might indulge himself. There existed, he thought, no valid reason why he should not call upon the Sandfords, merely in the hope of learning that they were about to leave Naples, or had given up all schemes for excursions into the country. It was just possible that the information which Galli had received was incorrect, though he was well aware from what Mrs. Sandford had told him, when they had met at Pompeii, that they had many such schemes under discussion. Still, it was not impossible that they had altered their intentions, and at any rate he would ascertain the fact.

Hoping, then, to find none of the party at home except Mrs. Sandford, in the course of the afternoon Noel presented himself at the outer door of the suite of rooms in which they were lodged. Before he had time to ring the bell, the door was opened, and Helen herself stood before him. She was looking bright and brilliant, and when a gleam of pleasure overspread her features as she recognised him, he thought he had never seen her so irresistibly winning and beautiful.

"Ah! Mr. Noel!" she exclaimed, giving him her hand, " there is nothing like repentance for one's misdoings. I am delighted to see you here at last. And now come in and tell me all the gossip you have been collecting since we saw you last. Everybody is gone out, and I was going for a dull and solitary walk, and you have just come at the very moment to enliven me."

Overpowered by her sudden decision and vivacity, Noel murmured a few words about his unwillingness to keep her indoors, and even offered to walk out with her. But Helen was in no mood for walking, and with a beating heart he found himself seated opposite to her in Mrs. Sandford's saloon before he well knew what he was doing.

"I am sorry to find Mrs. Sandford is not at home," he remarked in a kind of hesitating, stammering way, which, joined to the look of fatigue upon his countenance, convinced Helen that he was seriously out of health.

"She is gone with my cousin for a long drive into the country," Helen replied, "but I did not feel disposed to go with them."

"But surely they are not alone," Noel exclaimed, in a tone of alarm which Helen thought quite unreasonable.

"Why not?" she asked, fixing her eyes upon him, in the hope of discovering some explanation of his strange looks and manner.

"I hardly know—that is—do you often go out upon long excursions?" he stammered out, already feeling that he was on the verge of saying something that could only have been suggested by the statement of Galli.

"Yes," she answered, "we do sometimes, and we are planning an excursion to Pæstum for some day next week. And if you had been in a more sociable mood, Mr. Noel, we should have asked you to be of the party."

He shivered so violently as she conveyed this seemingly harmless information, that she was perfectly satisfied that he was about to be seriously ill. The information however, was so purely her own work, though he was conscious that he had put the question which had led up to it, that he thought that he might without scruple continue the subject.

"Of course you do not," he said, "that is—are you generally without companions? I fancied Mr. Evelyn was a good deal with you, and Della Porta was with you, I fancied, when I met you at Pompeii."

"They are both of them with my mother

and Margaret to-day," said Helen, in her turn wondering whether he detected the reluctance with which she heard the Marchese's name mentioned.

"Della Porta is a good and honourable man," observed Noel, resolved that his own misery should not prevent him from bearing testimony to the merits of the man whose lot he envied with all the intensity of his nature. He had also heard from Mrs. Sandford during their stroll in Pompeii, how courageously the Marchese had behaved in seizing the runaway horse, and had modified the somewhat contemptuous feelings with which he had hitherto regarded him as a mere aristocratic dandy.

"That I always thought him," Helen answered, unable to say more and looking fixedly upon the ground.

Convinced from Helen's manner that the Marchese was now her avowed lover, Noel found it impossible to resist the impulse to gaze earnestly at the features he so profoundly loved, as she still kept her eyes fastened upon the floor. As he watched her, the hot blood bounded through his veins and his whole frame thrilled with passionate fervour, till in a single moment he felt as if it streamed like an icy torrent from his heart. The hideous picture which had haunted him on the previous evening rose up in all its horror before his imagination, and as he saw the image of Helen writhing in the arms of the wretches whose crimes he was powerless to prevent, he ground his teeth in his agony, and clasped his hands together with a gripe of deadly force.

As he made no reply to what she had said, and continued silent, Helen at length looked up and was terrified at the frightful pallor of his countenance and the look of terror in his eyes.

"Mr. Noel," she cried, "what is it? You are dangerously ill. Pray tell me what it is, that I may do something for you. You are going to faint, Mr. Noel. Or what is it that gives you that deadly whiteness?"

"Oh, my God!" he exclaimed, in a feeble voice; "let me die! let me die!"

Frightened beyond measure at his looks and his words, Helen started to her feet, and seizing a glass of water which happened to be near her, held it to Noel's lip and earnestly bade him drink it. He drank a few drops, but she saw that he could with difficulty swallow them.

"Let me call some one, Mr. Noel," she continued, "and send for a doctor. You are not in a condition to be left to yourself; indeed you are not."

"No! no! no!" he cried, with inexplicable vehemence. "Send for no one! For God's sake send for no one!"

"But you are certainly on the point of fainting," she persisted; "at least, try what this will do for you." And she offered him the never-failing *eau de Cologne*, but his hands trembled so violently that he could scarcely hold the flask in his fingers.

"Come," she continued, "you are too ill to do it for yourself." And pouring some of the sweet spirit into the palm of one of her hands, she dipped her fingers into it and began bathing his forehead, seamed as it was with the effect of the agony he was enduring within.

To her affright he sprang to his feet the moment she touched him, and cried out—

"Oh, no, not that! for God's sake not that!"

A horrible suspicion darted into her mind. He must be mad. What else could account for such frantic wildness and such a haggard look of terror?

"What is it, then, Mr. Noel?" she could only say. "I implore you to tell me what I ought to do. You will be losing your senses if you put no better control upon yourself."

"I *am* mad already," he cried, with fearful energy. "Oh, Helen! Helen! would to God that I had never known you!"

Not understanding what could possibly be his meaning, but still believing that his mind was affected, Helen lost all power of action, and sank back upon her seat again.

"Mr. Noel," she replied, forcing herself to speak calmly, "what is it that you mean? What have you been doing that you talk in this excited and dreadful manner?"

"I have been loving you with all my heart and soul—almost more than God himself," he cried, the avowal bursting forth from his overcharged heart.

"Is this madness, or is it the truth, Mr. Noel?" Helen exclaimed, now in her turn pale with terror and dismay.

"It is madness and it is also the truth," he cried. "God forgive me for it, and help you to forgive me for it also. Year after year I have fought against it, and thought I had conquered it. It was for this I fled from Rome, and for this I have never been near you since you came here. I have struggled to tear every thought of you from my heart, but in vain. I know you can never be anything to me, for I am doomed to loneliness by a law that I cannot break, but yet I am maddened at the thought of your belonging to another. Oh, Helen! Helen! forgive me for the insult, for the crime, for the sin! Do not spurn me, do not scorn me in my misery. Only pity me in my wretchedness, and forgive me."

"I *do* forgive you, Mr. Noel," she replied; "from the depth of my soul I forgive you. But why did you come here to-day, when you knew that we might meet, and this terrible confession might be wrung from you?"

"I did not intend to see you, Miss Sandford," he rejoined, striving hard to be calm; "I wished to see your mother only."

"I will tell her what you were anxious to say to her, if that is what you wish," she replied.

"I had nothing to say," he returned;

"that is, I wanted to discover—I had something on my mind—oh, my God! shall I tell her?" he went on, with frantic passion, "will it be a deadly sin? Must the innocent suffer and the guilty go free to their hellish work? Yes, it must be done, if my own soul perish for the sin. Helen! Helen!" he continued, seizing her hand wildly, "for your sake and your mother's I am going to break my vows, and trample upon everything I hold most holy. I must do it, though I see the eternity of torment that is before me. Helen!" he exclaimed, clasping her hand with terrific violence, "there hangs—" and then he paused, and dropped the hand that he had been holding.

"No!" he began again, while Helen sat before him, speechless with terror, and vainly striving to interpret the meaning of his wild words and of the horror-struck looks that accompanied them. "No! not to-day! God help me, and help you also! It is not necessary to-day, and He may save me from this awful sin! But oh, Helen! my love, my life! I would die for you if I could save you from—but as yet I dare not speak the word," he added, in a low and hollow voice.

"Mr. Noel," Helen answered, as soon as Noel had done, "I am utterly in the dark as to the meaning of those passionate exclamations of yours, but you must permit me to remind you that it is an insult to me to say one word more upon the feeling which unhappily you have cherished towards myself."

"No, not cherished!" he exclaimed, "I have struggled night and day, and year after year, to destroy it. And after this hour I will never see you more. For one thing, at least, I am thankful. I never betrayed myself to you, and you never returned my feeling; at least, so I fervently hope."

"Never, Mr. Noel," interposed Helen; "no suspicion of such a thing ever crossed my fancy, and I never felt towards you except as a friend."

"Thank God for that!" Noel exclaimed.

"One question only I must put to you in return," Helen replied. "It will be a satisfaction to me to learn whether your secret has been communicated to any third person."

"Only to one person," he said.

"Is it fair to ask who that one person is?" said Helen.

"The Cameriere Giovanni Rinaldo," he replied.

"What conceivable reason can you have had for choosing that incomprehensible man for your confidant?" she asked.

"I did not choose him," Noel said; "he discovered my secret himself."

"Then perhaps he will betray you," exclaimed Helen, foreseeing, as she thought, fresh complications in the troubles she saw before them both.

"Never," he answered, with a confidence

which encouraged her to go on with her questions.

"Then you know enough of this strange person to enable you to trust him more than other people do," she suggested. "Who and what is he?"

"Who and what he is I cannot tell you," rejoined Noel, "for I know no more than you do, and yet I trust him implicitly. It was he who insisted on my leaving Rome, the moment he had penetrated my miserable secret."

"Has he any secret design of his own, do you suppose, which might make him wish you out of the way?"

"I do not believe it. He is an inexplicable man; but yet I trust him," Noel replied.

"Has he anything to do with those dreadful words you spoke just now?" asked Helen, hesitating, and yet filled with a burning desire to discover whether his frantic confessions of his own temptation to some terrible guilt were anything more than the creation of an over-wrought brain.

"Nothing whatsoever," he replied.

"One word more, Mr. Noel," she pleaded, as he was about to leave her. "This terrible danger that you say hangs over us all—is it very near at hand? You must understand how fearful has been the shock to me, and it is cruel to leave me shuddering in dread of some unknown misfortune. For God's sake tell me some little more before you go."

As she ended her appeal, he glared at her with a look of terror as if she were exercising upon him a deadly fascination from which he strove to shrink and fly, but all in vain. For a few moments he seemed as if he were on the point of yielding, and she would scarcely have been surprised if he had flung himself at her feet, and poured forth every secret of his soul in a tumult of conflicting passions. Then the expression of blank despair with which he closed his eyelids, as if physically unable any longer to endure the contest, told her too plainly that for the present at least he was incapable of saying more. Herself more and more overpowered with a vague and heart-sickening dread, she could only watch him in silence, as he slowly regained sufficient strength to walk totteringly to the door. Then he turned once again, and the look of unspeakable misery with which he regarded her before he disappeared, served only to deepen her conviction of the terrible nature of the troubles which he foresaw, but which he dared not reveal.

CHAPTER V.

NOEL IN HIS DESPAIR.

It was not far from noon on the following morning, when Evelyn strode up the dingy staircase of the house in which Noel was at present renting a couple of rooms. He had come to inquire after Noel's health, having been alarmed by the account which Helen had given of his condition, when her mother and the rest of the party had returned from their drive. She had, of course, said nothing of the real nature of the communications which had passed between them, and Evelyn was half inclined to hope that Helen's kindheartedness had exaggerated the symptoms of illness which her visitor had exhibited. Helen herself, however, displayed so painful an eagerness to hear whether Noel was worse or better, that he had gladly undertaken the duty of making enquiries.

As it was, Evelyn cherished the hope that he would find that her fears had been groundless, and he was preparing himself for a half hour's lively chat, and was resolved to overpower Noel's resolution to refrain from visiting his English friends during their stay at Naples.

Having with some little difficulty found out which were Noel's rooms, stumbling into two or three others on the way, and speedily retreating before the sights which met his eyes, and the odours which greeted his nostrils, he knocked twice without receiving any reply. The landlady, whom he had encountered at the entrance, had assured him that Noel was at home, and when he had knocked a third time, and no answer was returned, he entered without scruple, with a rising fear that something was seriously wrong.

When his eyes rested upon Noel, he was fairly startled by what he saw. Noel was sitting upright at a table, on which were lying several open books, with sheets of paper upon which he had apparently been writing, and as Evelyn involuntarily glanced at what was before him, it seemed to him that they were partially covered with wild and reckless handwriting, which even to the writer himself would be practically illegible. As Evelyn came forward, Noel took no notice of his salutation, but began turning the papers over and over, as if in search for some passages that he could not find. His face was almost of the hue of a corpse, and he looked twenty years older than he had appeared when Evelyn had last seen him. His restless eyes wore the unnatural brightness of fever, and Evelyn, not without experience in such matters, saw in a moment that, from whatever cause, Noel was lightheaded, and was not conscious of what he was doing. His hair was rough and dishevelled, and his whole appearance satisfied Evelyn that he had not undressed during the night, and probably had not slept.

Recognition, Evelyn saw, was not to be expected, and without saying a word of the purpose of his call, he spoke to him apparently without any surprise at the condition in which he found him.

"Can I help you in what you are looking for?" he asked, as if the request were the most natural thing in the world.

"Thank you, no," replied Noel, "I am sure it is here, but no one must see them. They are questions, Mr. Evelyn, questions of morals, which it is my duty to study and place before competent authority in a difficult case. Oblige me by keeping your eyes turned away, while I gather them up."

So saying, he eagerly swept the papers together. Then he began again.

"But you are a priest yourself," he said, turning to Evelyn; "why are you dressed like a layman? Suppose you are called to hear a confession," he added, with a look of sudden terror and a lowering of his voice, "and the man proves to be——"

Then he paused and trembled with affright before he spoke again. When he did speak, it was with passionate rapidity. "Bear witness," he exclaimed, "that I have said nothing; my soul is clear from the guilt! I have kept the secret, though I die for it, and they die for it, too!"

Totally unable to master himself so as to frame such questions as might possibly soothe Noel's agitation, Evelyn could only strive to repress his own distress at what he heard and saw.

"And how is Miss Sandford this morning, Mr. Evelyn?" Noel continued, with a vacant gaze. "Pray tell her that I was sorry to be so unfeeling towards her when she called yesterday, and that she need not be afraid, for I will make all straight for her. She can but die once, you know, and it will soon be over. Were you ever attacked by brigands before, Mr. Evelyn? They are devils alive, these Neapolitan murderers; and of course you will be one of the first to be shot."

Before Evelyn could force himself to reply, the landlady of the house walked hastily in.

"His reverence is no better, Signore," she began; "and it is my belief that he has neither eaten, nor drunk, nor closed his eyes since yesterday morning."

"He is very ill, I see that plainly enough," he replied. "Has no doctor been to see him?"

"What nonsense are you talking?" interrupted Noel. "Abstinence is necessary for severe study. Would you have me draw up my important questions with a clouded brain? My dear Evelyn, the woman is out of her senses."

"There is a man below who wants to see his reverence," said the landlady to Evelyn, without noticing Evelyn's words. "It is old Tolomeo, the sacristan, and he will take no refusal."

"Tolomeo!" cried Noel, with a sudden access of dread. "Oh, no, never! never! It is he who brought him. He called him a saint, but he is the blackest devil out of hell. And do you know," he continued, laying hold of Evelyn's arm familiarly, "he ran away. I looked round, and he was gone. If you could find him he would give me leave to tell, and we should all be happy again."

At a gesture from Evelyn the woman left them, and immediately returned in company with Tolomeo, who came in, terrified and scared. The moment Noel saw the sacristan, he seized him by the shoulders and exclaimed—

"Tolomeo, if you will bring him again, I will give you a thousand ducats. Do you hear, man? A thousand ducats, or ten thousand if you want them; and my friend, Mrs. Sandford, will give you as many more."

Not having heard how terribly Noel's mind was shaken by fasting, sleeplessness, and mental agony, the bewildered sacristan took his words quite literally.

"I am sure, your reverence, that I would do my duty without payment at all. But if your reverence is really disposed to make me a little present, in case my search should be successful, it will be a charity to a poor old man who will soon be fit for work no longer."

Then dropping his voice so that the listening landlady should not hear him, he added, with a significant glance, "Send her away."

Evelyn instantly took the hint, and dismissed the woman on some trifling pretence, and then took up the subject himself.

"Mr. Noel is not a rich man," he said, "and is at present very unwell, but Mrs.

Sandford will, I may safely say, be glad to make you a present, if you have any information which you possess and which Mr. Noel wishes for."

" Will his *eccellenza* say that name again?" returned Tolomeo, again catching the very word that he had overheard when listening to Noel's cries and prayers in the solitude of the gloomy church.

" The Signore is most gracious," he resumed, when Evelyn, greatly wondering, had repeated Mrs. Sandford's name to him.

" And is there no Signorina Sandford?" he further asked.

" Certainly there is," Evelyn answered, still more surprised, and remembering how grievously distressed they had found Helen after her interview with Noel. " There is the Signorina Helen Sandford. But what of that, my good friend?"

" And his reverence is not at all in his usual good health?" asked Tolomeo, too cautious to admit that he had any special reason for his inquiries. " Nevertheless, perhaps he could state what would be the amount of the little gift which he would bestow on me out of the fulness of his heart."

While all this was passing Noel had sat still, gazing into vacancy. Then he began murmuring to himself in broken sentences.

"Yes," he said, "there I am safe, and there will be no sin. He did not tell me that; I saw it with my own eyes—why did he go?—where is he? I looked to where he had been kneeling, and he was gone."

"Who is it you are speaking of, Noel?" Evelyn asked him, tenderly, and gently laying his hand upon Noel's arm.

"I?" Noel replied; "I spoke of nobody. It was Tolomeo who brought him, and told me he was a saint, and I found he was an incarnate devil instead."

"Where do you live, Tolomeo?" interposed Evelyn, resolved to have a private interview with the sacristan with the least possible delay, but masking his intention with a pretence that he might have to bring him some message from Noel in the course of the day. Tolomeo took the hint, and having given his address to Evelyn, he departed, well satisfied with the result of his cautious queries and suggestions.

"And now, my dear Noel," exclaimed Evelyn, satisfied that the first step towards Noel's recovery must be the simple act of eating and drinking; "you are in a most inhospitable mood this morning. I have had a long walk, and you offer me nothing to eat or drink."

"A thousand pardons!" cried Noel, completely convinced of the truth of Evelyn's words. "Let me call that old woman and send for a breakfast instantly."

Rejoicing in the success of the scheme, Evelyn was out of the room before Noel could stop him, and quickly reappeared, bringing with him some fruit, bread, and wine. As Noel showed no inclination to share the meal, a fresh thought struck Evelyn's mind.

"Is this the best description of bread that you get in this out-of-the-way quarter?" he asked; "taste it, and tell me if it is what they generally give you."

Unconscious of the trap which Evelyn was setting for him, Noel took the offered crust, and ate it. "I see nothing wrong," he observed, musing. "The bread is fair enough."

"It must have been my own fancy. I must try your wine, to get my palate into better condition."

Then after drinking a glass full, he added, "It certainly must be my fancy, for the wine seems odd in flavour also."

"Is it?" said Noel, innocently, and drinking the glassful that Evelyn poured out for him.

"At any rate there is no adulteration in these oranges," Evelyn went on, "at least it can hardly be worth their while, even in this land of swindling and duplicity."

So saying he cut up a plateful of the tempting looking fruit, and eating a slice himself, pushed the rest to Noel. " The Neapolitan oranges are only tolerable at the best, to my mind," he observed. "Do you recommend these as a fair specimen?"

Noel once more took the bait, and so grateful was the juicy fruit to his parched and thirsty lips, that before long he had largely helped Evelyn to clear the plate, Evelyn all the while contriving to keep up a sort of discussion as to its quality. To his infinite relief, the frightful brilliancy of Noel's eyes began to grow dim, as he went on eating and drinking, his features slowly assumed a more natural, though exquisitely weary expression, and the slight meal was scarcely ended when he fell into a heavy slumber.

For hours Evelyn sat there and watched the sleeper, ever on the alert to support him if he shewed signs of falling. As he still slept on, Evelyn ventured on the bold step of removing the books and papers on which he had been employing himself during his fit of partial delirium. Noel could but ask for them, if on waking he noticed their absence, and it was quite possible that if he woke in a more natural condition of mind, he would have forgotten their very existence until recalled by some chance suggestion. Without hesitation, therefore, Evelyn piled them together and placed them in a closet, out of sight.

When at length Noel awoke, Evelyn saw in a moment that the feverish glare in his eyes was gone, and that the light-headedness was succeeded by a distressing languor and sadness, which could only be the result of some intense inner struggles and misery. At the sight of his visitor he started, and would have risen from his chair had not his strength failed him.

"Mr. Evelyn?" he feebly exclaimed. "I was not aware—surely you bring no bad news—have you been long here?—I must have been sleeping for hours, I fear."

"I called by Mrs. Sandford's wish," replied Evelyn, "to ask how you were to-day; and I did not like to disturb you. We were sorry to hear from Miss Sandford that you seemed far from well yesterday."

"Ah! yes!" said Noel, pressing his hand to his head, "I remember now. I have had a good deal of anxiety on my mind, and am a little knocked up. Pray tell them that I am better."

"Well, my dear fellow," rejoined Evelyn, "you know best yourself how you feel, but to tell you the truth you look deucedly done up still, and if I were you, I would see somebody about it."

"Not yet! not yet!" returned Noel. "Has any one been to see me, do you happen to know?"

"None but a strange looking little old man," said Evelyn, "he called himself the sacristan, I fancy, of some church or other."

And after a little more such talk, during

which Evelyn extracted from Noel a promise that he would send for him, if he again fell ill, Evelyn left him, resolved to hunt out the old sacristan before returning to give his report to his friends.

CHAPTER VI.

THE SACRISTAN AT HOME.

WITH considerable difficulty Evelyn discovered the sacristan's dwelling-place. He found him lodged in a small room, which served at once for bed-room, sitting-room, and kitchen. A combined odour of dirt, onions, and stale sausages seemed to have taken possession of the walls and such scanty furniture as belonged to its inhabitant, flavoured with a smell of incense, constituting altogether a combination without precedent in all Evelyn's many wanderings in the worst smelling cities of Europe.

Tolomeo was, in fact, engaged in the preparation, or rather the adulteration of the composition of fragrant gums which is burnt so freely in the services of the Roman church. The manufacture of the incense in use at *San Pietro della Croce*, was a privilege conceded to the sacristan by the parish priest, by way of adding a trifle to the small salary which was attached to his office, and it was Tolomeo's practice to add still further to his gains by substituting coarser materials in the manufacture, in the place of those specified in the recipe which he undertook to follow. Living as he did in an atmosphere of nearly universal deception and cheating, he was well aware that even if he had acted honestly in this respect, nobody would have given him credit for it; and like the majority of the rest of the world, he repudiated altogether the unpractical notion that virtue unrewarded was worth cultivating for its own sake.

When Evelyn entered his room, he found the old man holding his hands over one of those little metal vessels which Italians, even of the highest class, employ for warming themselves when the weather is cold and damp, as it often is, even in Naples. His cunning little eyes seemed to be sparkling with a light which Evelyn could hardly suppose to be their usual brightness, and his crafty lips were curved into what seemed a very genuine, though by no means agreeable smile. He was, in truth, pondering over the fragments of information which he had picked up when he had discovered Noel alone in the church, and which were now supplemented by the actual names of some of the persons which he had heard Noel utter, in his unconsciousness that any listener was near. He was, moreover, expecting Evelyn to call, having detected his surprise at the condition in which he had found Noel, and surmising that where there was manifestly a secret to be ferreted out, the rich English gentleman would be as eager for its discovery as if he had been only a poor Italian, dependent for his living on the priesthood. As Evelyn came forward, Tolomeo rose and saluted him respectfully.

"I trust that the English padre is much better," he began. "Does his eccellenza bring me any orders from his reverence?"

"None whatever," replied Evelyn, by no means pleased with the man's elaborate servility of look and tone. "I hope he will soon be himself again. Can you give me any idea when it was that he first became so ill?"

"How should a poor man like me know anything of the ways of his reverence?" replied Tolomeo. "I did not learn that he was ill until I saw him this morning."

"But yet you seemed to be aware that Mr. Noel was anxious for some information that you could give him," said Evelyn.

"Did I, eccellenza?" asked Tolomeo. "It must have all flown away from my memory, for as you see, I am but an old man, and all the day I have been occupied in preparing the incense for Sunday next."

"And you wished to learn something about the names of certain English ladies," Evelyn continued.

"Ah, yes!" replied Tolomeo, "I do remember now. Some book it is, I think, that the English padre was wishing to meet with for his English friends—a very rare book, which they would pay handsomely for. Yes, yes! I recollect it all very well now."

Almost deceived by the look of simplicity with which Tolomeo uttered the ingenious falsehood, Evelyn thought that perhaps he had better say no more. It was, however, by no means a part of Tolomeo's plan that his visitor should leave him without communicating what was essential to his next move; namely, Mrs. Sandford's address in Naples. When Evelyn, therefore, showed signs of going, the crafty sacristan resumed the conversation.

"Yet now, I bethink me, Signore," he observed, "it was not a book that his reverence and the ladies wished for. It was something in the way of ancient church ornaments. Was it not some chalice, or cross? Our Neapolitan ears do not always understand the Italian words of foreigners, and that is why I asked for the name of the English ladies. I have a friend who deals in old silver; in a very small way it is true, but it is these small dealers who find the old-fashioned things that the foreigners seek for. He lives near the Chiaja, where the rich English mostly settle themselves; and if I knew the address of the friends of his reverence, I could desire him to take whatever little treasures he has, for their inspection."

The story about the dealer in question was another pure falsehood, invented on the spur of the moment, but it seemed so plausible, and the very non-Neapolitan character of Anglo-Italian pronunciation being so incontrovertible a fact, Evelyn fell into the trap, and without hesitation mentioned the number of the house on the Chiaja, where Mrs. Sandford was lodging. Nevertheless, he was confident that Noel, in his half-delirious talk, had spoken as if it was no mere book or rare piece of silver workmanship that he was so eager to discover. There could, of course, be no objection to giving the address of a lady which could have been learnt at a dozen places in Naples, by any one who chose to ask for it. But that, whether or not Tolomeo was playing the trickster, Noel was vehemently desirous of communicating with some living man, in whose discovery he thought that the Sandfords had an equal interest, Evelyn remained as convinced as before.

"Then you cannot recal any person whom Mr. Noel would wish to see, and whom you could find for him?" he said to Tolomeo.

"None in the world, Signore," said the sacristan. "His reverence has visited our church for only a few days, and he is busy about the registers—what for, I cannot tell. Only he is wonderfully curious about old matters, that had better be let alone."

To all further examination the cunning old man remained impervious; and Evelyn hastened to relate to his friends the result of his inquiries.

Left again to himself, Tolomeo's inward chuckle slowly expanded to something like a broad grin, as he pulled out a dirty prayer-book from beneath a heap of plates, knives, and crusts of bread, in an equally dirty cupboard, and on a blank leaf at the end of the volume wrote down the address of the English people from whom his cupidity expected a handsome gift. Then throwing the book back into the place from which he had taken it, he betook himself to his meditations.

"Of course," he said to himself, "it is Lorenzo Galli that he wants to see; and there is some secret between Lorenzo and the English padre. So now, Tolomeo, use your wits well, and put money in your purse, Tolomeo. But this Lorenzo is the very devil himself, with all his conversion. Ah! if one could but hear his story that he told the padre, and that drove the padre wild about it. Twelve murders! *Gesu! Maria!* what an infernal villain! And he is to come here this very night; but perhaps it is all a snare for me, and that young she-devil is playing a trick upon poor old Tolomeo. Ah! Tolomeo! Tolomeo! you have been a rogue in your own days, though you are the sacristan of *San Pietro della Croce,* now. Well! well! if Lorenzo does come, it is but to keep my tongue within my teeth, and listen with a thousand ears; and if he does not let out some little word or so to help me to his secret, and the padre's secret, and the English ladies' secret, then, my friend Tolomeo, you are an ass, and deserve to be well scourged. So now I will say fifty Ave Marias to San Antonio, and he will help me to worm out what Lorenzo wants to keep in the dark."

The pious operation being duly performed, with the mental addition that the saint should have one dozen candles burnt in his honour when his feast day next came round, provided only that he would move the heart of the ex-brigand to unfold itself to his devout "client," Tolomeo patiently awaited the coming of the perpetrator of twelve murders in a more comfortable frame of mind. When at length a knock at the door announced the expected visitor, Tolomeo's heart began to beat unpleasantly fast, but trusting to San Antonio and his own acuteness, he contrived to put on what he considered a pleasant expression of countenance as he welcomed his formidable guest.

The ex-brigand was clearly in no amiable mood, and his only reply to Tolomeo's humble salutation was a demand for wine. Excuses and falsehoods, as Tolomeo well knew, would be useless, and being eager to propitiate his visitor, he brought out a bottle of such wine as he was himself in the habit of drinking.

"Bah!" cried Galli, as he tasted the thin, sour liquid. "You thieve to small purpose, my friend Tolomeo, if this is the best stuff you have for your drinking."

"It is the very best I have," said the other, meekly. "If you will search my room through and through, you will find no better."

"Then go and buy something fit for a decent man to drink," Galli replied, "instead of standing staring with all your eyes, like the fool you are. There," he added, throwing a dollar upon the table, "and bring some supper besides."

"One should always profit by one's opportunities," observed Lorenzo to himself, as soon as Tolomeo had departed on his errand. "I dare say it is true enough that he has nothing fit for a good Christian like me to drink; but he may have other little trifles worth laying one's hand upon, nevertheless."

So saying, Lorenzo proceeded to institute a rough search through all the sacristan's few possessions. One of the first objects that caught his eye was the dingy little prayer book in which the sacristan had just written the Sandford name and address.

"Eh!" he exclaimed, "what have we here? What? does this old scoundrel pretend to say his prayers? And why not? It was only yesterday that I was turning devout myself, till that mad young priest brought me to my senses. I wonder how he relished his unexpected locking up. What's this, too?" he went on, with a sudden increase of interest. "In pale ink, too; just written, as I live! Ah! my friend Tolomeo, is this your game? Who the devil put you up to writing down the house where these English women are to be found? What? you are on the scent, are you? Well, my pious old worthy, we will eat and drink and make ourselves merry, and then we will square our accounts, Tolomeo. A little good wine will open those ugly little lips of yours, my good Tolomeo; and if not, why then—"

The savage smile with which the wretch muttered these last words aloud, as he placed the tell-tale book in his pocket, boded ill indeed for the fate of the sacristan; but when Tolomeo appeared with the supper, all trace of passion had vanished from the face of his guest, who insisted upon his sharing the feast with a joviality which quite captivated him.

"Come," he exclaimed, pouring out a couple of glasses of the coarse, heavy Sicilian wine, of which the better qualities are known in England by the name of Marsala; "here is a drink fit for a man, and not for priests and old women, my friend Tolomeo. "Drink this glass off, and warm your shivering bones."

Nothing loth, the sacristan obeyed, and by the time the supper was ended, his brain, unaccustomed to the stimulating liquor, which took no effect upon Lorenzo's hardened nerves, seemed precisely in that condition which was most favourable to his guest's designs.

"I had no notion," said Galli, pulling out the little prayer-book from his pocket, "that you were so piously inclined, my good Tolomeo. You are a sacristan, and yet you are positively given to praying! What wonder shall we see next?"

"Why should I not keep a prayer-book for other people's use as well as my own, Signor Lorenzo?" returned the sacristan.

"Ah! well!" cried Galli, shrugging his shoulders. "The nearer the church the farther from God; that used to be the saying in my young days. And a prayer-book, too, is handy for putting down any little trifles one wants to remember— eh? friend Tolomeo?"

Notwithstanding the fumes of the wine Tolomeo's legs began to shake, as he fully understood what these words implied.

"And who is this Mrs. Sandford, now living in splendid apartments on the Chiaja?" Galli went on. "She must be an English miladi, by her name. And what is it that makes you so careful about that admirable lady's address?"

"What address can you mean, Signor Lorenzo?" asked Tolomeo, with a clumsy air of ignorance.

"Ah! yes!" rejoined the other, "of course you lent this little book to some pious stranger, who came for her devotions to the church which has the advantage of your services; and she it was who kindly wrote her name in it before returning it to you. Yes! yes! I understand exactly."

Partially sobered by the sneer with which Galli spoke, Tolomeo began mumbling something about the friendship between Noel and Mrs. Sandford.

"But how comes it that it should be so important that you should be charged to preserve the address of his reverence's friends?" asked Lorenzo.

"His reverence is very unwell, Signor Lorenzo, and he might wish to send me on a message to his friends," said the blundering sacristan.

"Oh! indeed!" rejoined Galli, as if grateful for the information. "And his reverence is ill, is he, my friend? Perhaps from having caught cold, when he was left locked up in your infernally damp church, by some thoughtless person at whom you and I, Tolomeo, can make a shrewd guess."

"I am sure, Signor Lorenzo," said Tolomeo, more and more frightened by the bantering tone in which he was being questioned, "that I had nothing to do with locking the door upon his reverence."

"Now, you old villain," cried Galli, suddenly changing his manner, and seizing the unhappy sacristan's arm in an iron gripe;

"you are trying in vain to put me off with your idiotic excuses. Tell me what made you write this English woman's name and address in this book of yours. Tell me truly, you wretched little fool, or I will knock the breath out of your body before five minutes are over."

"I am sure I did not mean it," stammered the miserable man; "I did not do it on purpose—and his reverence did not mean me to hear—that is, he did not see me come in—"

"What?—you villainous eaves-dropper!" cried Galli, starting to his feet in undisguised fury, while the unhappy Tolomeo sat shivering and cowering before him. "What have you heard? Tell me all, or you know what comes next;" and he touched the handle of the long knife that was thrust into his waistband.

"Oh! Signor Lorenzo!" cried the shuddering wretch, "for the love of God spare me! I only heard something about the English signora."

"And that is all you want me to believe, is it?" said Galli, with contemptuous bitterness.

"That is all, I swear to you, Lorenzo," muttered the other.

"There was not a word about me, was there?" cried Galli, with a look that Tolomeo felt to be reading his thoughts through and through.

"Only a word or two," stammered Tolomeo, "and they meant nothing—indeed I heard no more—Lorenzo! Signore! I swear by God and the Madonna, that is all!"

In an instant Lorenzo's knife was in his hand, and lifting it over the quivering limbs of his victim, he seized Tolomeo by the throat, and held the frightful blade over his heart.

"You lie! you infernal perjurer!" he cried in a storm of fury. "You were listening while I was confessing to that Englishman, and you shall not leave this room alive. Now repeat to me every word that you heard, or I will tear your cursed flesh from your body, before this knife goes into your cowardly heart!"

With a sudden wrench Tolomeo freed himself from Lorenzo's grasp, and prostating himself on the ground, clasped his enemy's knee, and poured forth a torrent of denials to this fresh charge, with the wildest cries for mercy at his hands.

"You lie! you cowardly traitor!" returned the infuriated Galli. "I will give you ten minutes to prepare for your death, and then I will send you to the devil you have been serving!"

In that brief ten minutes all the sins of his wretched, superstitious and criminal life crowded up before the miserable man's imagination. Of great crimes he had not been guilty, his whole career having been one of petty thefts and endless falsehoods and swindlings. Above all, his innumerable

THE SACRISTAN AT HOME. 129

acts of what he had been taught to regard as sacrilege, stood out as the chief enormities of which he was guilty. Thefts of small sums given to him for the priests; falsifications in the accounts kept by him in reference to the expenses of church functions; an occasional abstraction of the trashy ornaments with which the images of the Madonna were decorated; and not the least, the purloining of certain parish registers in which he had been concerned, and about which Noel had been questioning him on the first day of their meeting. Ever since that day he had been inventing some scheme for restoring the missing documents, of which, in truth, he had made a list when he stowed them away amidst a huge collection of lumber, in a place to which he had intended to direct Noel, if only he could obtain a pledge that no harm should come to him from the discovery. These were the chief offences upon his conscience, and his horror of death was all the more overwhelming, because he believed that to die without being absolved from the guilt of these sins against the church, was to die without hope of Divine mercy.

As he knelt, or rather crouched upon the ground, thus shuddering in his agony, the brutal rage of the murderer, who stood watching him, gathered fresh force as each instant passed away. For courage, or manliness, or bloody crime, or savage cruelty, the man of many murders would have felt some sympathy or even admiration; but contempt for the coward and the petty thief wrought no pity and no mercy in a heart long familiar with every sort of bloodshedding, and he gnashed his teeth with impatience as the moments wore on.

He was on the point of bidding the unhappy wretch rise up from the ground for the purpose of being once more questioned, when Tolomeo again threw himself at his feet, and implored him to believe his words.

"No! you damnable and cowardly traitor!" cried Galli, dashing him away with all the force of his strong arm. "You have lied all your life, and do you expect to be believed now? You have been hearing what passed between me and that accursed priest; and you shall die. Yes! and so every traitor that comes across me shall die!"

And so crying, he deliberately knelt down on one knee, seized his wretched victim by his hair, and forcing his head backwards, drove the knife straight into his heart. There was no need of any second blow; but the murderer was resolved that his security should be doubly sure; and again and again he plunged the bloody steel into the still quivering corpse.

CHAPTER VII.

ON THE ROAD TO PÆSTUM.

AFTER another almost sleepless night, Noel was sitting solitary in his room, with a look of blank despair upon his countenance, and unable to come to any conclusion as to his duty and responsibilities. He had been again consulting one treatise of casuistry after another, vainly seeking for some case of conscience like his own, and hoping to find some justification for so far breaking what is termed "the seal of confession," as to warn his friends of the deadly peril in which they were involved.

At times the frightful picture of Helen

struggling for life and freedom in the hands of the brigand troop rose up before his imagination, and the heavy drops that streamed from his forehead told the anguish which he was enduring. Then, again, he nerved himself to cast all considerations of ecclesiastical obligations to the winds, and broke out into frenzied imprecations upon the system which held him in its ruthless bondage. To this would succeed the profoundest sense of self-reproach, and wild passionate cries for forgiveness of the guilt which he held that he was incurring by the mere harbouring of such rebellious thoughts. That his brain would give way under this frightful tension he was already beginning to be afraid; and to all his previous sources of anguish was thus added the further dread lest at the very moment when some opening might be offered by which he could save the woman he loved without violating his obligations as a confessor, his own reason would be already shattered for ever.

Already he was beginning a sort of wild calculation as to the length of time during which he might hope to preserve his faculties unimpaired, when all his thoughts were turned in a new direction by a visit from two officers of the city *gensdarmerie*. Their story was rapidly told. The sacristan, Tolomeo, had been found murdered on the floor of his own room, and the murderer had not left a trace behind him. The police were already on the search, and were making enquiries of all the other inhabitants of the house in which the slaughtered man had lived. But in the mean time, it was considered right that Noel himself, as the representative of the parish priest, should take charge of the bulk of the humble possessions of the unfortunate sacristan until some relations might be found to claim them.

Horror-struck at what he heard, and inwardly convinced that the supposed ex-brigand was in some way concerned with the murderer, Noel hurried off in company with the gensdarmes, forgetting for the moment his own distress in the presence of this fresh crime. He found the murdered man's room in the possession of the police, who were using actual violence to prevent the agitated crowd in the street and upon the staircase from forcing themselves in. Already it was whispered about that the notorious brigand Lorenzo Galli had been seen loitering in the neighbourhood for some few days past, and the sympathies of the district were pretty equally divided between the supposed murderer and his victim.

It required no long investigation to enable Noel to separate the sacristan's property into two divisions, one of them to be handed over to the custody of the police, the other to be retained by himself in his official capacity. He refused to take charge of any portion of the purely personal property, but took possession of all such trifles, whether papers or otherwise, which were in any way connected with the ecclesiastical offices which Tolomeo had filled, both in connection with *San Pietro della Croce,* or any other church to which he had formerly been attached. Among the rest, a few tables of marriage and burial fees, memoranda concerning parish registers, with scraps of old letters, attracted Noel's attention as probably bearing upon the very duties on which he was himself engaged. In his present misery all thought of these duties was laid aside, but with a vague and faint hope that he might some day be able to resume them, he mechanically put aside the papers in question before joining in the inquiries which were instituted with the view to discover the wretched sacristan's murderer.

Not the slightest clue, however, could be found. Lorenzo Galli had unquestionably been seen haunting the neighbourhood for some days past, and he was now no more to be seen. But not the most trivial fact could be brought to light for the purpose of connecting him with the murder; and not all

Noel's own feverish ingenuity could imagine any motive for his enmity against Tolomeo. On the contrary, he remembered with what exultation the sacristan had called his attention to the devout emotions which Galli had exhibited in the church, and the earnestness with which he had insisted on Noel's receiving the man's confession. Intense, therefore, as was his own personal desire to meet with the ex-brigand, he was forced to conclude that the murder of the sacristan was the work of other hands, and must be set down to the malice of some unknown enemy of Tolomeo.

When this conclusion was arrived at, Noel settled down into his hopeless misery with a more blank and helpless gloom than ever. The investigations of the police were quickly completed, and within four-and-twenty hours the sacristan's body was buried, and his memory was beginning to be forgotten. The Neapolitan populace are familiar with bloodshedding; the assassination of an obscure and friendless official was too trifling a matter to make any lasting impression in a quarter where criminals of all grades were looked upon with no severe reprobation; and it seemed the most natural thing in the world that a stranger priest like Noel should give himself very little trouble on so common-place an occasion.

Nothing, accordingly, occurred to rouse him from the fearful condition of stupor into which he felt himself lapsing. Saturday and Sunday came round, and no tidings were heard of Galli, and the doom of Helen and her friends seemed inevitable. All power of exerting himself, either in mind or body, seemed passing away. He slept hardly at all; but sat night and day, gazing vacantly before him, scarcely conscious of anything but that his faculties were giving way. The wild delirium into which he had at first been tortured returned no more. He could not rouse himself even to write or send a message to Evelyn, who had called upon him at the time that he was out of doors occupied in the investigations consequent upon the murder, and had naturally inferred that Noel had recovered from the agitated condition in which he had found him. On the Sunday he was not required to take any part in the church services of the day, for which other arrangements had previously been made. No one, therefore, except his landlady, was aware of his prostration, and she could do nothing but shrug her shoulders and utter endless ejaculations, and inform him that unless he would eat and drink he would unquestionably die.

Late on the Sunday evening she entered his room with the information that a poor peasant from the country wished to speak with his reverence and would take no refusal. Noel was already reduced to a state so near stupefaction, that he could make no reply, and the woman proceeded to introduce the visitor, who waited in silence to see her take her departure, and then made sure that she was not listening outside, before addressing Noel. He was dressed in the ordinary costume of the *contadini* of the Abruzzi, and until he had ascertained that there would be no eavesdropping, he moved with the slouching gait of the stupidest of the peasantry and kept his hat upon his head.

Then his demeanour totally changed. He sat down opposite Noel, uncovered his head and threw open his dress so far as to display the handle of what seemed a formidable dagger or knife. At first Noel had scarcely turned his eyes upon his visitor and looked so utterly unconcerned at his movements that the man was not a little confused, and knew not how to begin.

"You do not remember me, Signore," he at last began, in a tone barely audible.

The voice, especially as it was subdued to the same quality in which alone it was familiar to him, awakened Noel's torpid faculties, and he hoarsely murmured—

"You are Lorenzo Galli."

The man's tremor was manifest to Noel, dulled as were his present powers of observation.

"They say the old sacristan Tolomeo has been killed," rejoined the man, in the same subdued voice.

"Yes," Noel answered, unable to say more.

"Did your reverence see him after the day you were locked into the church?" asked Galli.

Striving to collect his wandering thoughts, and dimly conscious that Tolomeo had been with him at the time that Evelyn had visited him, Noel said he believed he had seen him, but was not sure.

"Then your reverence does not remember what the lying scoundrel told you?" said Galli.

"He told me nothing," Noel replied. "Why should he? But I am too ill to recollect."

"He might have told other people what he had heard," Galli cautiously suggested.

Noel's look of surprise convinced the man that whatever secrets the dead sacristan had revealed, they had not reached the ear of Noel himself.

"Who do they say killed him?" asked Galli, after a pause, and unable to repress the shudder with which he spoke.

"No one knows," replied Noel, now as agitated as the miserable murderer himself.

"Why should any body want to kill him?" asked the man, after another pause.

"No one knows," again Noel replied.

"Had he made any one his enemy?" asked Galli, still seeming to hesitate for words, and keeping his face steadfastly turned away from the look with which Noel was regarding him.

"No one knows," Noel said for the third time.

"Had he betrayed any man's secrets?" asked the other.

"I never heard that he had," Noel said.

Upon this the man rose from his seat, and laid two gold pieces upon the table that stood near.

"Those are for masses for his soul," he said, "I will see your reverence again tomorrow morning."

So saying, he folded the coarse wrapper which he wore close around him, pressed his huge hat over his forehead, and was gone before Noel could utter a word to detain him.

When the landlady returned she found Noel again in his former state of nervous excitement and ill-concealed terror, though free from all light-headedness. She noticed that he had drank off the wine which she had placed within his reach, and was alarmed at the suspicion that he was in the first stage of violent fever. But to all her enquiries he made no reply, only desired her to bring up the man who had just left him the moment he re-appeared on the following day.

Left to himself, Noel began that unceasing pacing to and fro, which resembles the restlessness of the caged wild beast, rather than the movements of a healthy active man. His brain was in a whirl, and all he could do was to ask himself why the infamous Galli should have supposed that his late victim had revealed the secrets of some enemy, who had avenged the supposed wrong by taking his life. That Galli himself was the murderer Noel was now abundantly convinced, but yet where was his motive to be sought? What secrets that concerned the wretched criminal could the poor sacristan have known and betrayed?

During the whole of that night Noel never closed his eyes; he strode heavily to and fro; he sat wearily in his chair; he threw himself at intervals upon his bed; but the one certain conviction that Galli had murdered the sacristan because he was in possession of some secrets fatal to his security, haunted him till it seemed burnt into his very brain.

All the while he was writhing under the hideous recollection that with the morning now at hand the doom of the woman he loved might be sealed for ever. That she would be safe until Sunday had come and gone, he had not doubted, fully trusting what Galli had told him in his self-deluding confession. When the day at last dawned, and he looked out and saw the sun rising in all its southern splendour, he reflected with horror that this very splendour might be now tempting Helen herself to prepare an early start upon the excursion which must lead to her destruction. Then, as the rising beams shone out upon the distant hills, whose tops he could just discern from his window, all exquisitely lovely in their forms, now glowing in the early radiance, the contrast between the heavenly beauty that he beheld, and the deadly agony within him, all but paralysed his exhausted heart, and he could only stagger back from the sight he saw, and fall upon his knees with cries to the God who made it all, to have mercy upon him.

It was not long before the man for whose coming he yearned, as offering the last faint hope of relief, presented himself in the same guise as on the previous evening. By daylight the countenance of the blood-stained wretch exhibited signs of a terrible conflict in his savage soul. At any other time, the indescribable mixture of alarm, suspicion, and reckless brutality which his features displayed would have struck Noel with bewilderment and disgust. At the present moment all that he desired was that the man should go on speaking in such a manner as to justify him in acting, without violation of his obedience as a priest, upon the information he had given him in the confessional.

For some minutes the man seemed striving to make the dialogue turn upon trifling subjects. When Noel's patience, however, was on the point of giving way, Galli spoke out the real thoughts of his heart.

"Is it true, your reverence," he said, "that you clergy sometimes betray the secrets of your penitents to the police?"

"God forbid!" ejaculated Noel, in his sincere horror at the very act to which, in another shape, he was himself impelled by a temptation against which he could scarcely stand.

"It is said that so it is," rejoined Galli, with a glance of savage suspicion.

"I never knew of it being done," Noel replied, with an air of candour that disarmed the villain before him, and encouraged him to come directly to the point at which he was aiming.

"*Signor padre Inglese,*" he said, "will you tell me the truth? Have you revealed one word of my confession to you, which you brought to an end by your senseless folly?"

"Not one word," cried Noel, with passionate vehemence.

"Will you swear it?" continued Galli.

"I will swear it," exclaimed Noel, instantly.

"Swear, then," cried Galli, springing to his feet, and seizing Noel's arm, "swear by God, and Mary conceived without sin, and all the saints, and all the devils in hell, that you never have uttered and never will utter one word of my confession to you."

"I swear," replied Noel, "by God and his mother, and all the saints, as I love them, and by all the devils in hell, as I abhor and resist them, that I have never uttered and never will utter one word of what you then said to me."

"If I bring any of my old friends to you, *Signor padre*," Galli continued, "will you swear the same to them about what I confessed to you?"

"I will, undoubtedly," Noel rejoined; "but why do you ask me this?"

"Because if they fail again in their plans against those English ladies, they will say that I betrayed them to you, and will have my blood before the sun goes down."

Noel's heart beat so furiously that he could barely draw breath to reply.

"What ladies?" he faintly asked, "and what plans?"

"Your English Sandfords," said the man, falling into the trap which he had set for his own feet. "I told you that they were to be carried off the first day they went into the country this week. To-day is the day, and if they fail, you will have my old comrades here to-night, and if you are alive at midnight, you will be a happy man."

In the twinkling of an eye, Noel dashed past the astounded villain who had thus thoughtlessly repeated the information which he knew that he had already given under the seal of secrecy. Seizing his hat as he dashed from the room, Noel was flying down the staircase before the horror-stricken Galli could recollect how he had committed himself. The streets were already alive with passengers, and the appearance of an ecclesiastic hastening wildly along, filled them with astonishment and curiosity.

Fortunately for Noel, he was soon hailed by the driver of one of the fast Neapolitan hackney carriages, lazily beginning to ply for hire. It was impossible, he thought, that the Sandfords could have already started, as he urged the man to put his horses to their utmost speed. Arriving at the house, he sprang to the ground, and bidding the driver wait, he bounded up the staircase, and rushed unannounced into the room where he had so lately parted from Helen in the anguish of despair. It was empty, and no sounds of voices greeted his ear. In deadly terror he called for Helen by name. Then he cried and shouted, till a servant came. They had been gone about half an hour, he told Noel, and he was not aware in what direction they had started, nor where they were going, only he did not expect them to return till the following day.

As he heard this knell to all his hopes, Noel groaned aloud.

"Perhaps his *eccellenza* the Marchese might know where the ladies are gone," suggested the servant, seeing Noel's strange agitation.

"Is he not with them?" exclaimed Noel.

"The English Signore only is gone with the ladies," said the man. "The Signore Marchese remains at home to-day."

Clearly there was nothing for it but to seek out the Marchese, and him Noel sought, overwhelmed with despair.

In the mean time, Mrs. Sandford and the rest of the party were enjoying the brilliancy of the weather and the beauty of the scenes through which they were driving. Evelyn, in his liveliest spirits, was assuring Helen that their friend Noel could not be suffering under any serious illness; and as soon as he had succeeded in quieting her anxieties, he proceeded to awaken all Mrs. Sandford's terrors by an elaborate narrative of certain brigand atrocities which he invented on the spot. Like a good many Englishmen, he really disbelieved five-sixths of the stories told about the extent of Italian brigandage, and no suspicion of any real danger crossed his thoughts. Mrs. Sandford, on the contrary, took all his extravagant stories literally; and it was only when he had confessed that they were every one of them the produce of his own imagination that she was content to proceed on their journey.

When they were about seven miles from Naples their driver pulled up at a small wayside inn, calling itself the *Albergo d' Italia*, to deliver a message with which he was charged to the landlord; and while the two men were in conversation, a handsome girl, apparently belonging to the better class of the Neapolitan peasantry, stepped forward, and coming up to the side of the carriage, asked Evelyn whether he could give her any information as to the proceedings of a certain Lorenzo Galli. He was her friend, she said, and had promised to send her a message or a letter by a party of English excursionists, which she might expect to meet at about that very hour.

"Lorenzo Galli!" echoed Evelyn; "I fancy I have heard the name. But no such person has given me any message or letter whatsoever."

Unwilling to turn away with no tidings of the man she called her friend, but who was in fact her betrothed lover, the girl stood still, looking disappointed and distressed. Then observing that the driver of the carriage and the landlord were still in earnest conversation, she asked in a low voice whether the Signore had heard anything more of the murder of the sacristan Tolomeo.

"Anything more?" exclaimed Evelyn;

"good heavens! what is it you mean? I saw him alive but a few days ago. Who has murdered him?"

The girl shuddered as she replied, "God only knows. But they have done talking, Signore," she added, with a glance at the landlord; "only, for the love of God, do not go further than the *Albergo del Re* to-day. It is about three miles further on."

"What in the world was that bold-looking girl telling you, Mr. Evelyn?" asked Mrs. Sandford, as the driver mounted his box and lashed his horses into a hand-gallop. "I can scarcely understand the Roman Italian; but as for this Neapolitan patois, it might be Greek or Hebrew to me."

To Margaret and Helen the girl's communication had been only partially intelligible, but what little they had understood of it made them watch Evelyn's features with painful anxiety as he replied to Mrs. Sandford's question. The forced smile and elaborate gaiety with which he spoke entirely failed to reassure them.

"She was expecting a message from some friend of her own, and seemed annoyed at receiving none," he said.

"But, Mr. Evelyn!" exclaimed Helen, "how came she to expect us at all?"

"That she did not say," he answered. "She seemed to think, too, that we should hardly get very far on our road to-day, which is a horrible nuisance. I had no notion the roads were so wretchedly out of repair."

"They seem extremely good at present," observed Margaret, satisfied that Evelyn was intentionally mis-stating what the girl had said.

"Well," he replied, "we can but go on as long as they continue what they have hitherto been."

For another two miles or thereabouts the journey was continued as easily as before, though a cloud had settled upon the spirits of the party, which all Evelyn's efforts at cheerfulness failed to disperse. Evelyn was beginning to wonder how far they were still distant from the inn which the girl had specified, when the driver again pulled up and announced that one of his horses had lost a shoe, and that he must unharness it and lead it on to the nearest inn, at which a blacksmith would be found. To Evelyn's remonstrances and arguments, proving that the horse could walk quietly forward in harness with the carriage behind him, the man returned a dogged "*Non possibile, Signore,*" all the while busily unbuckling the harness of the unshod steed. When he further proceeded to unharness the second horse, Evelyn would stand it no longer, and gave the man to understand that he would resist him by force.

"The Signore may do as he pleases," he retorted, "the horses will not bear being separated; and the ladies must remain where they are, or walk back to Naples."

"Take that one horse forward, you scoundrel!" cried Evelyn, "and unharness this other at your peril."

"The Signore is not my master," rejoined the man, with an angry scowl, as he again began to unbuckle the harness of the second horse.

"For God's sake, Charles!" cried Margaret, in her terror, "let the man alone. He will think nothing of stabbing you, if you interfere with him."

Yielding to Margaret's entreaties, Evelyn bethought himself of another kind of device.

"Come aside with me, my friend," he said to the driver, in a more conciliating way. "Let us have a word or two about this between ourselves."

The man obeyed the summons, and walking a few yards ahead, Evelyn began again:

"I see your game, my friend," he said, looking straight into the man's eyes. "Name your sum for driving us back instantly to

Naples. Your horse can do well enough without his shoe, if it pleases you to make him."

Instead of giving a direct answer, the man hesitated, and then replied—

"Does the Signore know who killed the sacristan Tolomeo?"

Completely taken aback by the question, Evelyn was only the more convinced that the man was playing a deep and deadly game. All he could say was that he was in utter ignorance on the subject. Then the driver took up the question that Evelyn had just put to him, mentioning all sorts of impossible amounts, but steadily refusing to come to a definite agreement. His whole manner was so evasive that the conversation was prolonged until Helen and Margaret both called out to learn when it would come to an end.

Before Evelyn could answer them, the sharp crack of a rifle rang through the air, and a bullet whistled within a foot of Evelyn's head. With a loud cry of pretended terror the driver instantly took to his heels, and fled. He was not out of sight, when half-a-dozen savage-looking men leapt over a low wall, which formed the boundary of a clump of trees, whose trunks were rendered impervious to the sight by a thick growth of underwood.

At the sound of the rifle shot, Evelyn had dashed back to the carriage, wherein sat Mrs. Sandford in an agony of horror, with Margaret and Helen only a little less overwhelmed with dismay. The men surrounded them in a moment, and one who seemed their chief laid his hand upon Evelyn's shoulders.

"*Signore Inglese!*" he said, with a movement of the brow that spoke of the relentless cruelty of his nature; "unless you are mad, you will make no resistance. These ladies will be good enough to come with us, and you yourself will return to Naples and make arrangements for their ransom."

"Never! never! never!" shrieked Margaret, throwing herself out of the carriage, and seizing Evelyn's hand with a look of burning entreaty.

"Never! never!" he replied; "we will rather die together on this spot!"

Then with a sudden wrench he freed himself from the grasp of the brigand who held him, and clasped Margaret around the waist with one hand, while with the other he drew from his breast-pocket the very pistol with which Margaret had once been so painfully familiar. The man paused as the weapon was presented to his head, but his companions uttered a shout of mocking laughter.

"All Englishmen are mad!" cried one of the number, "and this *milordo* is as mad as the rest of them. We are six of us, and he would frighten us as if we were children."

While he spoke, another of the band crept quietly behind Evelyn, and flinging his arms about his neck, held him helpless in his gripe. But in the struggle, Evelyn's revolver was fired, and the chief of the troop fell bleeding upon the road. At the moment that he fell, a sudden cry broke from a third miscreant.

"Too late!" he almost screamed aloud. "Again too late! The soldiers are upon us, and we are betrayed!"

It was true enough. The clattering of horsemen, and the ring of a musket-shot fired into the air, announced that help was at hand. The brigands and their intended victims turned instinctively in the direction whence the sounds struck their ears. A troop of a dozen mounted carbineers were dashing on at the utmost speed to which they could urge their horses.

"Fly for your lives!" cried the wounded chief, still prostrate on the ground; "and whether I live or die, remember the traitor."

He had scarcely spoken when his comrades fled like scattered vultures from their prey, and when the soldiers came up to the carriage, the wounded captain of the band was the only prize that remained for their capture.

"God be thanked for this!" ejaculated the Marchese, darting forward from the troopers, by whose side he had ridden, from time to time entreating the officer in command to urge them to a speed in reality impossible.

As he shook the hands of Evelyn and of the still affrighted ladies, he could with difficulty restrain the tears to which in his warm Italian temperament he would have naturally given way in the ecstacy of his joy. Refraining, however, from that un-English expression of his emotions, he turned to one of the soldiers, and bade him, with his superior's leave, gallop back to the little *Albergo d' Italia*, and tell the English *padre* that all his friends were safe.

Then he told the story of the rescue. Frantic with agitation, and breathless with fatigue, Noel had called upon him for instant help, telling him the peril that hung over them. Happily, he himself, through his acquaintanceship with one of the chiefs of the Neapolitan police, was able to secure the immediate services of a troop of mounted carbineers. Borrowing a couple of horses from the officers of the regiment, Noel and himself had ridden in company with the soldiers, but on reaching the *Albergo d' Italia*, Noel's strength had completely given way, and he had been carried almost lifeless into the inn, and left in the charge of one Agnese Bruno, whom Evelyn quickly identified with the girl who had described herself as a friend of Lorenzo Galli. To Helen's eager inquiries Della Porta replied that he was convinced that on hearing of their safety, Noel's strength would revive, and that he would soon be himself again.

It was speedily settled that after all that had happened it was out of the question to think of prosecuting their pleasure scheme. The unharnessed horse was caught, and

11—2

Della Porta, mounting the box of the carriage, drove the party back to Naples. At the *Albergo d' Italia* they rested awhile, while Evelyn and the Marchese satisfied themselves as to Noel's condition. He was still too prostrated in strength to be removed; but as soon as the Sandfords and Evelyn were quietly in the carriage together, the Marchese busied with the whip and reins, Evelyn told them that haggard, worn, and still agitated as they had found Noel, there was an ineffable look of peace and gratitude settled upon his features which no words of his could describe.

The girl Agnese was sitting in the room with him, herself overpowered with some secret misery. Noel had asked him to send out some conveyance for him before the evening, and had begged him to provide a lodging with some respectable woman for the girl Agnese, whom he would in all probability bring with him to Naples. "There is some terrible secret involved in the poor girl's history," Noel had said; and she ought not to be left in the charge of such doubtful hands as those of the landlord of the inn and his family. The officer in command of the troopers had undertaken to leave a guard in the house for the rest of the day; and Noel and Agnese might therefore be left without risk until the evening.

With this assurance they proceeded on their return in peace.

CHAPTER VIII.

D'URBINO'S EYES ARE OPENED.

WHILE the quiet which the Sandfords and their friends had sought at Naples was thus terribly interrupted, D'Urbino's perplexities, both in regard to Francesca and his wounded guest, grew more and more serious. Many days passed before Rinaldo was sufficiently recovered even to think of his being removed to his own home. In the mean time, from some inexplicable fascination, D'Urbino's interest in his uninvited companion continued steadily to increase. The painful sense that he was being watched for some unexplained end, began sensibly to diminish, as his confidence in the sincerity and uprightness of Rinaldo's character was strengthened by the necessary intercourse which now passed between them. The presence of the sick man in the studio was now scarcely felt to be an intrusion, and D'Urbino was surprised to find how much there was to be learnt from the criticisms of a cultivated, but non-professional observer.

The singular mixture of feelings with which Rinaldo regarded the nearly finished head of Francesca was the chief puzzle which was presented for his ingenuity to solve. His eyes were perpetually turning in its direction, sometimes with a look of irritation prevailing over the look of pleasure with which he clearly regarded it, and sometimes with an appearance of unalloyed enjoyment. "I can't make that girl out at all," he observed one day to D'Urbino, after a long study of the features of the portrait; "but I wish you were not obliged to see so much of her as you now seem to be."

"My dear Cameriere," replied D'Urbino, in the friendly tone which was fast becoming habitual with him; "you must allow me to say that you are most unfair to Giorgione's daughter."

"Is she Giorgione's daughter?" replied Rinaldo. "That is just the question."

"Why in the world should you doubt it?" asked D'Urbino, a little vexed at Rinaldo's persistency about his *protegée*, as Francesca was now fairly constituted.

"I cannot tell you," said Rinaldo. "Without the slightest reserve I may say that I cannot tell; but I do doubt it nevertheless."

"But why should you care about it at all?" returned D'Urbino.

"There again," said Rinaldo, "I hardly know my own mind. All sorts of things come into my head, as I lie here; and this is one of them. I do wish to know for a certainty that Francesca is not that man's child, and I very much more earnestly wish that you would not treat her so much as an intimate acquaintance."

"Here again you mystify me," rejoined D'Urbino. "Why on earth should you concern yourself about my acquaintanceship with Francesca, or with any body else?"

"There is this one reason, at any rate," said Rinaldo, with that strange tenderness and humility which always disarmed D'Urbino, even when most vexed at his guest's perverse allusions; "I owe you the safety of my life, through your goodness in suffering me to stay here, to your own great discomfort."

"The discomfort is a trifle," D'Urbino answered; "and as you now talk of removing in a day or two, you must permit me to take the opportunity of saying that it has brought with it a very real gratification in enabling me to understand you better, and to regard you with sincere respect."

One of Rinaldo's rare but exquisitely happy-looking smiles lighted up his worn features, as he listened to what D'Urbino said. It passed away, it is true, as rapidly as it came, but all through the rest of the day, although he seemed lost in thought, and scarcely spoke at all, there was perceptibly less sadness in his face, and when he moved, it was with far more ease and comfort than he had exhibited since the infliction of his injuries.

As to the relations of D'Urbino and Francesca, they were daily changing their character. Her distress and difficulties, arising from her father's continued absence, were such that it was impossible that D'Urbino could neglect her; while the imperative necessity for keeping the discovery of Donato's proceedings a secret until Giorgione should return, rendered it impossible that any third person should be taken into their confidence. Hence it came about that he saw her daily, and that before long she unfolded to him her suspicions that her father was involved in some trouble with the government authorities.

By degrees, too, as day after day went by, and no hint was given by her father as to the period of his return, while he carefully avoided compromising her by letting her into the secret of his place of concealment, her suspense and wretchedness grew intolerable. Thus, too, she insensibly became more open in her manner towards D'Urbino. All her resolutions that she would never, if possible, see him again, and that when compelled to meet him she would confine herself to the discussion of matters of urgent necessity, gradually dissolved into the feeblest of struggles against an irresistible destiny.

Restless and weary with the dreamy speculations and fears engendered by living alone in the house, with no companion but one of the dullest of servant maids, how could she help waiting and watching for the daily visit of one to whom her whole heart was given, even though it was madness to cherish the passionate affection? How could she check the smile on her lips and the sparkle in her eyes, when she heard him enter the house, whose solitude since he last left it had been so unsupportable?

> "His very step had music in't,
> As he came up the stair."

Besides, every now and then there was the trembling but sweet hope that in the possible changes and chances of the uncertain life of Rome of to-day, some happy complications of affairs might bridge over the social gulf that separated her from the man she had dared to love. She hated herself for the thought, but still it would recur again and again, that if she could not rise to his position, she would welcome his descent to her own, as the greatest of possible blessings. It was base, she said to herself, it was cruel, it was insulting, it was selfish beyond pardon, that she should harbour such a thought for a moment; and whenever it nevertheless revived, and she could not fling it away in indignant self-reproach, she would fall on her knees and pray passionately that at any cost such traitorous hopes might be rooted out from her heart.

All this while, D'Urbino's sentiments towards the poor girl were slowly taking a new tone. Being a man wholly without conceit, though proud almost to the verge of haughtiness, it never occurred to him that the lovely girl whom he was befriending entertained towards himself any feelings warmer than those of gratitude and good-natured regard. He therefore did not dream of doing her any injury by bestowing on her so much of his companionship and conversation, even in circumstances so perilous, at one of the most susceptible periods of a woman's life. Francesca Giorgione, he had always thought, so far as he had thought at all on the matter, at two-and-twenty years of age, was not likely to make a fool of herself by throwing her heart away without cause upon any body; and when now and then he had imagined her marrying some man in her own sphere, the only reflection which followed was to the effect that he should thus lose a remarkably valuable and companionable aid in his pursuit of living art.

Even now that he found his own interest in her becoming daily more warm, and detected his thoughts wandering towards her at all kinds of unexpected hours, he was as far as ever from reflecting that unless he made up his mind, in one way or other, he might be inflicting upon her an irreparable and unpardonable wrong. When for the first time he asked himself whether he should propose to her to marry him, and then instantly scouted the idea as absurd, he made no question but that she would rejoice at the proposition, simply as an arrangement for her own comfort and advancement in life. To refuse an offer to which she could have never pretended in the ordinary course of Roman life, would, he took for granted, be an act of folly which would be impossible to a girl of so much sense and strength of character, while her father's authority would have at once put such a refusal out of the question.

Thus it came to pass, that he entertained no scruple in paying his repeated visits to Francesca, partly with the *bonâ fide* purpose of arranging any difficult matters which might turn up during her father's prolonged absence, but quite as much for the pleasure of her company. No harm could come of it, he felt assured, except perhaps to himself. If he should ultimately find himself, as his friend Evelyn expressed it, seriously "hit," it was but to deny himself the gratification of her society, and his wound would quickly heal;—unless indeed;—and then the faintest glimmerings of a meditation on the possibilities of his marrying her, *coute que coute*, would arouse and startle him from his dreamings.

In the meanwhile, it would undoubtedly

be for the advantage of Francesca herself that she could derive such little cultivation from the talk of a man of more accomplishments than she could pretend to. And so he went on from one little advance to another, first of all lending her a book, beginning with the great Italian novel of our generation, and when Manzoni was ended, taking her a selection from the comedies of Goldoni. One afternoon he went so far as to read aloud to her. The excuse that he made was the manifest unfitness of some of Alfieri's tragedies for the study of a girl, still ignorant of the terrible realities and crimes of human life. So, partly for the pleasure of the reading, partly for the sake of observing the effect of some of the great poet's most affecting passages upon her sensitive organisation, the volume went backwards and forwards in his pocket between his own and Giorgione's abode more than once and more than twice.

The readings from Alfieri were, in fact,

still going on, when they were brought to an end by a rude interruption. Rinaldo was still a tenant of D'Urbino's studio, his recovery proving far slower than was expected. His doctor declared his belief that the shock to the general constitution had been severe, and that supervening upon the exhausting effects of a life of care and trouble, a second shock would probably be more than the enfeebled vitality of his patient could bear.

Returning from one of these Alfieri readings, expecting to find his guest in his ordinary mood of grave meditation or turning over the leaves of one of his own sketchbooks, he found him in a state of distressing agitation.

At first D'Urbino could draw from him no explanation of his condition. Then yielding to repeated entreaties, Rinaldo avowed that he had been thrown into the profoundest trouble by some information which had just reached him, and that he was torn with doubts as to the course of action he should adopt in consequence of it. His sense of duty and his personal inclinations were alike divided, and prostrated as he was by illness, the struggle was overwhelming. To D'Urbino's urgent appeals for further enlightenment, and protestations that he could give no advice while kept in the dark, the sorely troubled sick man still made no direct reply; but after a while, resting his head upon one of his hands and closing his eyes, he extended the other hand to D'Urbino, who was sitting by his side, and for the first time called him by his Christian name.

"*Fioravante mio!*" he began. D'Urbino took the proffered hand, which was all the answer that Rinaldo required.

"The villain Donato has been here while you were away," he continued. "But let me tell you without interruption," he added, as D'Urbino, now abhorring the ruffian more than ever, since his feelings towards

Francesca had assumed their new warmth, received the information with a passionate imprecation.

"He has been at large ever since that memorable night, and learning that I was here, and that you were not within, he came with an old story, cringeing and fawning upon me, and begging me for the love of God to forgive him."

"The infamous hypocrite!" muttered D'Urbino.

"He is that, indeed," pursued Rinaldo, "but now he is on a new tack. Knowing the post I hold in the household of his Holiness, he took it for granted that I should rejoice to learn that he has now turned informer, and that he has offered his valuable services to the government, undertaking to betray the best kept secrets of the insurgent side. He is not satisfied with the payment offered by the police officials who manage the dirty work of this sort, and in particular he is savage because Colonel Bastiani treats him with the personal contempt that he deserves. He clearly thinks that he still has some hold upon me, or some claims upon me, and he believes that I shall stand his friend. Like every rogue, he holds every man to be as deep a rogue as himself."

"Well," replied D'Urbino, "how does this lead up to the sources of your agitation? In all this, I see nothing that need cause five minutes' hesitation."

"You will now see," rejoined Rinaldo, "I was able to hide my anger and my intense annoyance and loathing, so far as to induce him to betray some little of the game he is playing. He was too cunning to show his whole hand, but he told me what are the chief baits which he is holding before the chief of the police. He has given them information about the mosaic-worker Giorgione, which has set them on the right scent after him—at least, so he says; and he protests that they believe him, and that by way of preliminary, there is to be a domiciliary visit at Giorgione's house very shortly;—of course to search for any letters that he may have written to the daughter, communicating to her his place of hiding."

As D'Urbino heard all this, his intense attention gave way to a feeling of uncontrollable alarm. Though well aware that Francesca's father had left her in the dark as to his abode, yet he knew that the annoyance she would suffer would be terrible; and as the search throughout the house would be complete, he foresaw that the police would pursue their examination beyond the barrier between the two adjoining houses, and once within Mrs. Sandford's house, who could foretel what would happen next?

"Of course this must be told to Giorgione's daughter without an hour's delay," he replied, when Rinaldo had finished.

"So it shall be," said Rinaldo, "and I thank God that I have not fought in vain against the temptation. *Fioravante mio!*" he went on with his look of child-like humility, "I have escaped a horrible sin. I was sorely tempted, my son—forgive me before I confess it, but I can hide nothing from you—I was sorely tempted to keep this information to myself, and to leave the man Giorgione to his fate."

"But not his daughter, Cameriere," interposed D'Urbino, with an enforced and terrible calmness: "not his daughter; say that you intended to spare his daughter."

"I wished to spare her, and intended to spare her, but the temptation to separate you from her by allowing her to be driven away to join her father, was very fearful. You forgive me, at any rate, my son?" he added, from the depths of his self-condemnation.

"I thank God, Signor Rinaldo, that your better mind has triumphed," rejoined D'Urbino. "And now, when you are rested, let us decide what is to be done."

For a brief space Rinaldo made no reply. Then in a totally different tone he began. "Look at me, Fioravante," he said; "look me in the face, and take heart to answer me, in the fulness of your sincerity and love of truth."

D'Urbino complied, and the frankness of his gaze encouraged Rinaldo to proceed.

"You love that girl, my son," he said.

"Ought I to be ashamed of it, if it is true?" he answered. "You would not be surprised, my good kind friend, if you had seen what I have seen of her."

"Do you think that she returns your love?" pursued Rinaldo.

"It never occurred to me," he replied, "that she cared for me in any way but as a friend, who naturally came to her at a very trying time of perplexity. At least, it never occurred to me till this very afternoon."

"And now?"

"Now I suppose it is the mere beginning

of a fancy, more gratitude than anything else."

"And what do you propose next?"

"I have been thinking that I have been a portentous fool, and something like a heartless scamp besides."

"How so?" asked Rinaldo.

"A fool, at least," he returned, "if I have been letting myself walk blindfold into love with a poor girl, notwithstanding her poverty, when I might not even have the satisfaction of finding that she would care for me, except as a stepping-stone to get on in the world."

"Come near again, and listen to me," said Rinaldo, D'Urbino having started to his feet in his annoyance.

He sat quietly down, and Rinaldo resumed—

"She loves you with her whole heart and soul!" he said, with a fervour that seemed to add to the amazement with which D'Urbino received the astonishing statement.

"You are jesting," he cried. "How is it possible that you should know anything whatever about her feelings? She never showed me the faintest shadow of any affection."

"She has shown *me* their reality," returned Rinaldo.

"Impossible!" cried D'Urbino: "it is utterly and preposterously impossible!"

"Then why did she spend hours after hours of the bitter winter afternoon and night, watching for your release when you were arrested after the riot at the Coliseum?"

"Who told you this?" asked the bewildered D'Urbino.

"I saw it myself," rejoined Rinaldo, "and I gave her refreshment when she was perishing with cold and exhaustion, and I sent her home to her father's house that night."

"Then this is the explanation of all that wretched mystery!" exclaimed D'Urbino, "and you have respected her secret ever since. What a wonderful girl she is! Poor Francesca! what she must have been suffering! and all from my abominable stupidity and blundering, and selfishness!"

"I wish she was not that man's daughter," resumed Rinaldo. "No good can be expected from a man who is mixed up with that infamous Donato. Why, the scoundrel has before this boasted to me that he often paid visits in the night time to this Giorgione, and passed hours there unknown to anyone. And from other information I was satisfied that the boast was not altogether false."

"Yet surely you are not repenting your resolution to save him," suggested D'Urbino.

"Not in the smallest degree," he answered. "If it were only an affair of politics, I might hesitate. But as this Donato has long been my worst enemy in the world, and the other man is his ally, I may look upon him also

D'URBINO'S EYES ARE OPENED. 187

as my personal enemy, and return him good for the evil he may have done me. You are surprised at the reasoning," he added, seeing how little D'Urbino was prepared for the practical conclusion; "but life for me will soon be ended, and it is time to learn to forgive."

D'Urbino could resist no longer. The greatness and the sweetness, and the simplicity of the noble heart that he was learning by degrees to comprehend and to love, overpowered every proud and angry thought. He flung himself upon his knees before the bed on which Rinaldo lay, and seizing his hand with true Italian fervour pressed it to his lips.

"Fioravante, my child," murmured Rinaldo. "I may tell you now, for now I see that you love me. There is a tie of blood between us, which will soon be known beyond dispute; and when I die, it will not be a lonely death."

"What is it?" asked D'Urbino, rising

from his knees, and comparatively calm again.

"It would be cruel to say more as yet," he replied. "A few days will set all my fears at rest; and at any rate I shall not lose your love."

CHAPTER IX.

GIORGIONE'S RETURN HOME.

AWARE of the extreme awkwardness of the position in which Francesca would be placed, if he made any avowal of his affection for her during her father's absence, D'Urbino confided to her only so much of this last conversation with Rinaldo as related to the communication made by Donato. Moreover, without being really convinced by Rinaldo's assertions concerning the complicity of the mosaic-worker in the villainies of that double-dealing scoundrel, he was haunted by an unpleasant suspicion that the relations between the two men required clearing up; and he was the more anxious for a speedy explanation of the connection between them, now that he had finally determined to throw hesitation and the customs of society to the winds, and to ask Francesca to be his wife.

The decision to which he came after informing Francesca of the impending visit of the police, was described in the letter which he hastened to address to his friend Evelyn at Naples.

"From the note I had from you, written three days ago, I gather the unwelcome conclusion that my letters are not always safe in the post-office, or that my messenger here has been playing me false. I have no time just now for repeating the news I sent you, as I am anxious to let you know what has just been happening of a most unpleasant kind. That scamp Donato whom we caught coming away from Giorgione's premises has, very unintentionally, been the means of bringing to my ears the intelligence that Giorgione's house is to be honoured by a domiciliary visit, in search of the absent owner's address. It seems that Giorgione is in hiding somewhere, and his daughter is in terrible distress altogether about the whole affair.

"Now for the more confidential part of my communication to you, as to which you must use your own discretion in respect to communicating it to any one of the Sandford ladies. I have been over every room in Giorgione's house, in company with his daughter, and have ascertained that on some night, or some day, not very long ago, a man and a woman, or possibly a man and two women, passed between the highest stories of the two adjoining houses, through a disused entrance, supposed by everyone to have been permanently closed by strong double doors. The footprints in the thick coating of dust which covers the flooring of Giorgione's story are not effaced, and tell the tale with irresistible force. They are not the marks of the shoes of Giorgione's servant; and the conclusion is manifest. Donato and Mrs. Sandford's servants are in league, and the vagabond was in some way or other prevented from carrying off the jewels and cash which of course he and the maids had plotted to get hold of.

"You will see at once that even if Giorgione's daughter takes my advice and effaces these footprints, the gensdarmes will be all alive when they come upon the old doors that I have mentioned; and then there will be the devil to pay. I should tell you that Francesca knows nothing as to her father's whereabouts; and therefore the police people will be so savage at the disappointment that they will make sure that here at last they are coming upon the secret.

"It strikes me that the right thing for you to do will be to ascertain whether the ladies have lost any valuables, and what are their ideas as to their servants' characters.

After this you will know what to do. Only above all things I must entreat you not to lose an hour in letting me know the facts of the case. There are reasons which I cannot give you without telling too long a story, which make me more anxious than I can say to have the matter cleared up before the police pay their promised visit; which there is every reason to expect will be on the day after to-morrow. Now farewell. I am off to post this letter with my own hands."

About noon on the following day, Evelyn entered the room where the cousins were sitting; discoursing on their own and their various friends' affairs, with D'Urbino's letter in his pocket.

"You look beaming with intelligence, Mr. Evelyn," exclaimed Helen, as he came forward. "What welcome news have you to enliven our dulness?"

"Is it the intelligence which is the characteristic of my own admirable mind, that you mean?" he replied, covering his anxiety with his much-loved banter, " or the intelligence which you assume that I am charged with in the shape of news?"

"I meant the former, of course," she replied, "but I see now that I ought to have inquired for the latter."

"Your penetration, as usual," he rejoined, "is not at fault. I have a letter from our friend D'Urbino, and for some absurd reason or other he wants to know whether any of you have lately lost any jewels or money? There is some well-known scoundrel about in Rome just now, and possibly they want to collect evidence against him."

"No!" said Helen. "I have lost nothing."

And Margaret said the same, adding that her aunt would certainly have spoken about it, if she had been the sufferer. As Evelyn hesitated to say more, Margaret took up the conversation.

"Is that all he says about it?" she asked.

"I don't know why I should not repeat what he says about it," Evelyn replied; "he seems to have a notion that your maids may possibly be scarcely honest."

"What can he possibly mean?" exclaimed Helen. "There is more behind, Mr. Evelyn, I see it in your countenance. Pray tell us all at once."

"After all, I may as well tell you why he asks, for he bids me use my own discretion about it. He has got it into his head that some persons, a man and a woman, or a man and two women, have been passing between your house and the mosaic-worker's."

The cousins turned to one another with looks of dismay, while the burning blush that overspread their features told Evelyn that here was some painful secret, far more distressing than any mere doubts as to the trustworthiness of maidservants. Tortured by the thought, he sat gazing at them in silence, when Helen rose up and led Margaret to another part of the room. After a

13—2

short private conference they returned, and Margaret took her lover's hand.

"We ought to have told you this before," she said. "It was to please the Marchese that we put off telling you till we were back again in Rome."

"Confound the Marchese!" cried Evelyn. "What on earth has he to do with it? Was he the thief in league with the maids?"

"Nonsense, Mr. Evelyn," rejoined Helen. "He was only so disgusted with our proceedings, that we promised to say nothing about them, till it was absolutely necessary."

"With your proceedings!" echoed Evelyn. "Then are you the midnight conspirators in league with Donato? Here is mystery upon mystery."

"Yes, Mr. Evelyn," said Helen, laughing, "I *am* one midnight conspirator, and Margaret is the other. But we were not in league with the real villain; rather we conspired against him, though we did not know that he and your scamp Donato were one and the same villain."

"The deuce you did!" cried he; "what a valuable wife I shall have, if ever England is overrun with housebreakers! But pray, Margaret, enlighten me as to your first efforts in the thief-catching line."

Margaret laughed, and turning to her cousin bade her tell the whole tale.

"That is because she wishes not to be the historian of her own heroism, Mr. Evelyn," said Helen.

"Nonsense, Helen," interposed her cousin; "you would have done precisely the same in my situation."

"There, my dear, you are most egregiously mistaken," replied Helen. "Mr. Evelyn," she continued, "have you happened to examine that little revolver of yours, on which you bestowed such an unaccountable amount of affection on the night before we left Rome?"

"Indeed I have," he answered, "and I

found that some person had taken the unwarrantable liberty of firing one of the charges."

"That charge was fired by this young lady," said Helen, pointing to Margaret, "in the face of the man Donato."

The look of Evelyn's face, as he heard this startling announcement, was simply indescribable. His eyebrows rose to a height almost incredible, while his lips gradually curved into a smile of intense enjoyment, and finally he broke into peals of ringing laughter, in which the cousins finally joined, not, indeed, at the recollection of their perilous adventure, but at the very unexpected mirth with which the story of it was received by the much astonished Evelyn.

After this, there was nothing for it but to describe everything in detail, and finally to go carefully through D'Urbino's letter. Then Evelyn broke out again.

"And now," he said, "I see what a benevolent destiny was guiding my own steps that night, and indicating that intensity of interest which indissolubly links my life with that of the heroine of the pistol. Scared and singed, the unhappy robber rushed out to his fate, and was struck down with a blow from my fist, as he attempted to escape from the consequences of his crime. There must be few thieves to whom it happens to be knocked over on the same evening by a young lady and by the gentleman to whom she will ultimately be married. I look upon this coincidence as furnishing the happiest augury for the success of our united efforts on behalf of the disturbed Francesca. If only we could introduce a few love anxieties into her affair, the parallel between the two cases would be complete."

"Had we not better decide what is to be done, and leave romancing to the future?" asked Helen, afraid of what Evelyn might say next.

In the end it was determined that the

three then present should start for Rome without a day's delay. Mrs. Sandford was to be persuaded to remain behind, and it was to be suggested to Della Porta that he would be playing the part of a friend if he would undertake to pay her all possible attention until she would join the others at Rome, or until they could return to Naples. If she consented, it would be possible, they believed, to reach Giorgione's house early in the following afternoon, and Evelyn undertook to telegraph to D'Urbino to announce their coming. Happily, Mrs. Sandford was in an obliging mood, and the cordial approval of her favourite, the Marchese, completely reconciled her to a proposition of which she was not allowed to know the real reasons.

On his way to make his own preparations, Evelyn encountered Noel, whom he had seen daily after his own and the Sandfords' narrow escape from a horrible doom. Noel's own health was still but partially restored, and he even talked of leaving Naples without completing the work on which he was employed; but for some inexplicable reason he had steadfastly remained in his solitude. Evelyn now stopped him and informed him of his own sudden departure, in company with Margaret and Helen, on account of the uncertainties of the Roman and Neapolitan post.

"You relieve me from some perplexity," Noel replied, after a little thought. "You won't mind taking charge of a small packet of papers, and finding some way of getting it safely into the hands of a man you must have heard of—the Cameriere Rinaldo."

"What, are *you* a correspondent of our mystifying friend?" asked Evelyn.

"It is simply a commission he entrusted me with," said Noel, "but he, or some friend of his, is in immediate want of the papers."

"If they are in my hands within an hour to-day," replied Evelyn, "they shall be in his hands before to-morrow night."

"So it shall be," said Noel, as they hastily parted.

Meanwhile D'Urbino and Francesca were in all the misery of prolonged suspense. He had convinced her of the absolute necessity of engaging an additional servant to remain in the house both night and day, so that on the first sign of the approach of the gensdarmes, some one might be at hand to summon him to her assistance. The peculiar character of her relation towards himself made him doubly anxious that no suspicion of secrecy should attach itself to his visits, prolonged as they sometimes were.

When Evelyn's telegraphic message reached him, his relief was immense, so far as it promised their speedy return. But at the same time, the mere fact that they had resolved on so sudden a measure, showed that their anxieties were very great, and that they were in possession of more information than he could possibly have expected.

Early on the momentous morning he was with Francesca for some time, and when he reached his home again, he beheld Rinaldo up and dressed. He was pale and feeble looking, but a strange light burnt in his eyes, and told the fact that it was no healthy vigour, but only the intoxication of excited nerves that lent him his apparent strength. He pointed to a message which the telegraph had brought him from Noel, as an explanation of the agitation which he vainly strove to subdue. It informed him that the papers he expected would be brought to him in the course of the day by a private hand. Confident that this could only mean that they would be brought by Evelyn, he insisted on accompanying D'Urbino to the house of Giorgione, and there awaiting the arrival of the travellers. "Besides," he added, when D'Urbino remonstrated against so hazardous and agitating a step in his present enfeebled condition, "my presence will ensure at least a civil treatment of the poor girl herself, and it may save her father's property from needlessly rough usage. This will be one good result of the influence I possess through the official post that I hold."

Remonstrance, in fact, was useless, as D'Urbino soon perceived, while he was well aware that Rinaldo would suffer far more from an enforced solitude at such a time than from any excitement which the dreaded search might produce upon his shattered system. The gain to Francesca, too, was not to be lightly rejected; and the arrangements once decided upon, there was every reason that they should run no risk of being absent when the police arrived.

It was not long after mid-day when they accordingly presented themselves at the door of the mosaic-worker's house. No opportunity having been allowed for D'Urbino's preparing Francesca for her unexpected visitor, her distress and disturbance were unconcealed. Rinaldo saw it all at a glance, and he therefore imparted an additional kindness into the words with which he greeted her.

"My dear child," he said, "I am come to throw myself on your charity for an hour or two. But now you must let me rest and say nothing, while our friend here explains for what purpose I am trespassing upon you."

The tenderness of the tone in which he spoke, and the fatherly look in his eyes, would have gone straight to Francesca's heart, even if his colourless cheeks and his enfeebled gait had not awoke her pity. She led him without reply into an inner room, and he lay down and watched her peaceably, while D'Urbino told what he had to tell. Then by degrees the anxiety of the three began to yield to a hope that the gensdarmes might not arrive before the travellers from Naples. These last could not by any possibility be with them before two o'clock, and in all probability it would be three o'clock, not reckoning of course by the old-fashioned Roman method of dividing the four-and-twenty hours, before they would drive up to Giorgione's door.

As two o'clock drew near, every sound that reached them from without aroused afresh the tumult of hopes and of fears within their breasts. It was Rinaldo's highly strung nerves that enabled him to detect the sound they dreaded, while Francesca and D'Urbino heard no more than the ordinary noises of the street.

"The soldiers are here," he faintly said. "D'Urbino, leave the child here with me, and go yourself to meet them."

As he spoke, he took her hand tenderly in his own, and held it, while D'Urbino obeyed him. D'Urbino left the door by which he went out wide open, and the clang of swords and carbines told the truth they so much feared to hear. Then a startled cry of astonishment uttered by D'Urbino was answered by a voice that drove the blood back wildly into Francesca's heart.

"It is my father himself!" she cried aloud, as she sprang forward to meet him. He was there, indeed, and surrounded by a party of carbineers, commanded by no less a person than Colonel Bastiani, with a couple of police officials in attendance.

Quick as thought she was in his arms, and locked in his embrace, while her agitation and terror found relief in a torrent of tears. The first to speak was Colonel Bastiani.

"Signorina," he began, "your father has done well in giving himself up of his own free will; and I will take care that his act is duly represented in the proper quarter."

She looked up in her father's face as she heard this, wondering if it could possibly be true.

"He speaks the truth," said Giorgione, replying to her surprised gaze; "I learnt something of the search with which you were threatened, and at all risks I felt that I must come and save you from the misery of enduring it alone."

"Then why are the soldiers here?" she asked, "unless," she continued, as the terrible future struck upon her thoughts, "unless it is to carry you away again to prison?"

"I grieve to have to tell you, signorina," interposed Bastiani, "that a fresh charge has been brought against your father, which it is my painful duty to see investigated. It is brought, it is true, by a worthless scoundrel, whose word is nothing; but he alleges that the charge can be proved beyond a doubt."

"Bring in the informer," he added, turning to his men, "it is high time to proceed."

A sergeant left the house, and immediately returned, preceded by the informer, Donato, in the charge of two additional policemen. The wretched man came in skulking and cowering beneath the Colonel's contemptuous glance.

"Your accusation is this," said Bastiani,

"that treasonable documents of a most grave character are to be found concealed in some part of this house, and that you were present when the master of the house concealed them."

"Eccellenza, it is so," returned Donato, gathering courage now that the importance of his position began to appear. "But I am guaranteed a free pardon for myself, as a reward for the information."

"You will of course be with us throughout the necessary search," said the Colonel to Giorgione, who bowed his acquiescence.

D'Urbino here stepped forward, and acquainted Bastiani with the presence of Rinaldo in the adjoining room, adding that he would confer a kindness on him if he would allow him a few words of conversation. Bastiani complied, and shortly returned to give orders for beginning the investigation. Francesca clung to her father's arm, as he led the way from one chamber to another, followed immediately by Bastiani, behind whom came the informer, in charge of the policemen, and a small detachment of soldiers. Rinaldo, supported by D'Urbino, followed last of all, while the remainder of the soldiers occupied the lower portion of the house and the courtyard in its rear.

CHAPTER X.

THE INVESTIGATION.

The investigation was conducted regularly from room to room and from floor to floor, with all the practised keenness of the agents of a government which habitually resorted to such odious measures for crushing the rebellious spirit of its subjects. Donato, indeed, at first remarked that so prolonged an investigation was useless, as he had never been present with Giorgione in any of these chambers. The remarks were of course disregarded, and Bastiani sternly desired the fawning scoundrel to hold his tongue, unless he had something definite to communicate.

For some time nothing whatsoever rewarded the searchers, and Bastiani merely observed that it was not likely that papers of a treasonable character would be carelessly stowed away in rooms regularly occupied by the members of any family. As they mounted higher his eyes followed more keenly the opening of every closet door, and the overhauling of the few articles of furniture that could by any possibility be made a secret depository for books or papers. As some fragments of manuscripts were found at the back of an old escritoire, he observed that the countenance of Giorgione wore a disturbed and sorrowing look, and after a glance at what was written, he carefully put the papers into his own pocket.

"What have we here?" exclaimed Bastiani, as at last they reached the highest story. "If we are to examine every one of these lumbering chairs and tables, we shall be here till midnight. Pictures, too! who does not know that there is nothing so full of deception as a picture frame? Cameriere," he went on, as Rinaldo, leaning upon D'Urbino's arm, with difficulty entered the chamber, "this is far too much for you. Lie down at once on this sofa, without stirring a step farther."

Rinaldo obeyed, and D'Urbino placed himself by his side, noticing, as he did this, that Donato spoke something in Bastiani's ear. To the surprise of every one, Bastiani immediately directed the whole of the furniture with which the place was crowded to be brought together and piled up in a corner of the room, in order that the walls might be laid completely bare. When all was clear, he desired one of the police to follow the usual custom of tapping all along the ragged plaster, on which the remains of former painting and decorations were still visible. For some yards the sound thus produced was of that dull, dead quality which is all that is yielded by solid brick or stone. Then suddenly every eye was rivetted upon a spot that returned a hollow murmur, and the man who struck it exclaimed that he saw signs of some rather recent repair of the stuccoed surface.

The Colonel stepped forward, while Rinaldo and D'Urbino studied the movements of the informer. The man was trying to restrain the signs of exultation which quivered upon his lips, and he clasped his hands together with nervous twitchings. A flat wooden board, covered and concealed by the plaster, was quickly extracted by the powerful tools brought by the police, and revealed a small hollow space behind, about a foot square. It contained a bundle of papers, which were handed to Bastiani. He turned them over, amidst the dead silence of all present.

"Diavolo!" he suddenly exclaimed, "what foolery is this? These are nothing but old tavern bills and fragments of newspapers, stained with wine and smelling of vile tobacco. What in the name of folly can have induced any rational being to make all this ado about hiding such trash as this? Nevertheless, they must be impounded," he observed, handing them to the sergeant in attendance.

All this while Giorgione had looked on with calmness, though Francesca noticed a perceptible tremor in his arm, as the wall yielded to the dexterous strokes of the man at work upon it. At the next sound of Bastiani's voice his tremor renewed, and Francesca could feel the throbbings of his heart.

"Try the floor immediately underneath that part of the wall," said the Colonel, after receiving a second hint from Donato. "It looks suspicious enough," replied the man at work, "now I examine it more closely. This board is positively loose, and the fellow who put it in its place deserves to be whipped for a bungler."

The board yielded without difficulty, and another bundle of papers was displayed, and placed in Bastiani's hands.

The Colonel's countenance fell as he turned them slowly over. Donato cautiously advanced a step or two, and attempted to see and read the papers without being perceived.

"Colonel Bastiani!" shouted D'Urbino from behind, "that villain is looking over your shoulder at the papers in your hands."

Bastiani turned sharply round.

"Lay hold of the scoundrel," he cried, "and if he moves again, put on the handcuffs."

"Signor Giorgione," continued Bastiani, "be good enough to step forward."

Giorgione came forward, grave and pale, but with a firm step and open countenance, while Francesca retreated to the side of Rinaldo and D'Urbino.

"A pen, ink, and paper," continued Bastiani.

"Be so good as to write a sentence or two," he went on, when the order was obeyed. "Anything will do. You may write the words of any treasonable poems if you like, for it will do you no harm, being done at my desire."

Giorgione complied.

"H'm!" observed Bastiani, when he read what was written. "Of course you say all this, but nevertheless I will take the advice. Now, then, to compare your writing with that of these papers."

Amidst a breathless silence Bastiani proceeded leisurely with his examination. He then selected three documents from the rest, and handed them to Giorgione.

"You do not wish to deny that they are in your handwriting."

Giorgione took them, and at once returned two of the number, admitting that he wrote them, but it must have been many years ago. The third perplexed him greatly. He turned it over again and again, and seemed still unconvinced.

"If you will allow it, Colonel," he said at length, "I will copy a portion of this document at the foot of the sentences I have just written."

"By all means," replied Bastiani, "though I don't see what you are aiming at."

Giorgione wrote what he wished. He then again examined the document which he had been studying, comparing it with the writing he had just finished. Returning the two manuscripts together to Bastiani, he begged him to allow a second examination at a further stage of the investigation, urging the terrible nature of the accusation that would now be made against him, stating that he hoped still to explain how and by whom it was brought forward.

"This next paper seems harmless enough," said Bastiani, handing a fourth manuscript, "but you may as well turn it over."

As Giorgione read it, he frowned angrily, and closed his lips firmly, as if striving to recal some forgotten event.

"You have the diary which was taken from me this morning by your orders, Colonel," he said. "May I ask you to open it, and turn to the entry of the tenth of October last."

Bastiani complied.

Again taking up a pen, Giorgione wrote a few words.

"Is this a correct account of the substance of the entry of that date?" he asked, placing what he had written in Bastiani's hand. "Do not, if you please, show me the actual diary, but simply say yes or no."

"It is perfectly correct," Bastiani replied.

Giorgione heaved a sigh of relief, and exclaimed, "I have now the key of the whole mystery."

Francesca interpreted aright the change in her father's countenance, and silently seized D'Urbino's hand and grasped it in the intensity of her thankfulness. D'Urbino returned the pressure, and a thrill of joy shot through the poor girl's frame, as he continued to hold her hand within his own.

"Yes," Giorgione went on to say, "it is a clue which must lead to the truth sooner or later."

All at once, after turning over the next leaf in the manuscript, his whole figure shook with an overwhelming agitation.

"Oh! my God!" he cried, "the villain has defeated his own ends! at last! at last! at last!"

He sank into the nearest chair and covered his face. Francesca sprang to his side, but he said not a word, only kissing her tenderly on the forehead. Quickly recovering himself, he rose and returned the paper to Bastiani, saying as he did so,

"Is there need of further inquiry, Colonel? of course you cannot accept my denial, even on oath, that I had no hand in placing these documents where they have been found. Nor can you accept my assertion that the third paper you showed me is a forgery. Your duty is to consign me to prison on the charge of having treasonable papers in my possession. I cannot as yet account for their presence here, and I am prepared to obey your orders."

"But I can account for their presence," cried the loud voice of a new comer.

And Evelyn, pushing the soldiers right and left aside, strode up to the spot where Bastiani and Giorgione were standing. He had been waiting for some time outside the room, with Margaret and Helen, watching the proceedings through the open door, and unable to find any means for communicating with D'Urbino without being observed.

Bastiani greeted him with a stately bow.

"Mr. Evelyn, I believe," he said.

"We have met once before, Colonel," replied Evelyn, "and under rather unpleasant circumstances. It is to the affairs of that very night that I have now the pleasure of directing your attention. Ah! my good friend Donato," he exclaimed. "You are here most opportunely to listen to my ingenuous narrative."

Bastiani smiled grimly at Evelyn's imperturbable coolness.

"Colonel Bastiani," continued Evelyn, "the papers you have discovered were placed in that hole that I see before me, on the night I speak of, by that vagabond's own hands."

"No doubt you have proof of this wonderful story, Mr. Evelyn," said the Colonel.

"You remember that on the night in question," pursued Evelyn, "Signore D'Urbino and myself gave that amiable gentleman into custody on the charge of burglary in this very house."

"You did so, but the charge was not substantiated."

"You remember also that the hair of the fellow's face and head was unaccountably singed and smelt of gunpowder."

"And further," said Bastiani smiling, "that he was adorned with a black and swollen eye, which report attributed to the strong arm of Mr. Evelyn."

"I can assure you, Colonel," replied Evelyn, "that I never in my life knocked a fellow down with such satisfaction as I experienced when I administered the facer in question to that very unprepossessing gentleman. But to return to the singeing. It was the result of the firing into his face of this very handsome little revolver by a person who surprised him in the act of depositing these documents in the place where you now have found them."

"And who is that person?" inquired Bastiani.

"That person is close at hand," rejoined Evelyn, "and I shall now have the honour of introducing that person to you."

Followed by the astonished looks of the whole assemblage, Evelyn passed through the door, and immediately reappeared, leading the blushing and trembling Margaret by the hand. Every sort of exclamation of amazement broke from the lips of the well pleased soldiery, as Evelyn presented Margaret to the Colonel, who received her with as undisguised a stare as his sense of politeness would permit."

"Colonel Bastiani," said Evelyn with all the formality of a master of the ceremonies, "I have the honour of introducing to you my friend Miss Osborne. So far as I can make out from the surprising narrative, Miss Osborne is now standing on the very spot where she shot that scoundrel in the face."

The colonel bowed his most gracious salutation, and then observed that he marvelled much at the man's escape with his life."

"There was only blank cartridge in the pistol, Colonel," said Evelyn, "but the fellow was knocked over backwards, and then took to his heels and fled."

"And am I to understand that Miss Osborne was the sole witness of this man's proceedings?" asked Bastiani.

"By no means," said Evelyn, "another lady, her cousin, who is now waiting to be presented to you, was her companion."

"Another lady!" echoed half-a-dozen voices from among the soldiers, with sundry subdued comments as to the incomprehensible and unparalleled character of English women in general.

Bastiani, indeed, was begining to think that the presence of so many strange men would materially interfere with the examination to which it would be his duty to subject these feminine and youthful guardians of the peace, and anticipating a request from Evelyn and D'Urbino, he desired the soldiers and policemen, with Donato in their keeping, to await his further orders in a room on the lower floor. Helen was then led in by Evelyn and introduced to the Colonel as Margaret's coadjutor in the detection of Donato's villainies. Between them they soon related all the circumstances which it was material should be known, and though they had not seen the papers actually deposited in their place of concealment, yet it was impossible to doubt the conclusion to which every circumstance pointed.

Giorgione was next examined as to the clue which he imagined that he had found, towards tracing out the history of the introduction of such papers into his house.

"For reasons entirely of a private nature," he replied to Bastiani's inquiries, "this man has for very many years had a hold upon me, which he has sought to turn to his own profit. And I have not the smallest doubt that he took the opportunity of my being absent from home, to introduce this bundle with the intention of obtaining a reward from the government, for the discovery in the manner in which it has now been made. He has often plundered me, and now finding that his game was over, he resolved to throw me overboard and turn informer.

"Now, too, I see how long he has been

scheming for this one end. It was he himself who induced me to leave my house on the day that I went away, and I have learnt from a friend whom I have in the department of the police, that it was he too who made the new charges, all utterly false, against me, which have kept me hiding until now. His object was to prevent my return until his end was accomplished. As to the three first papers you gave me, two of them are of old date and implicated me in matters on which I have long ago made my peace with the government of Rome. The third is a forgery. I was confident of it when comparing it with the handwriting of the two others; but wishing to convince you that though professing to have been written quite lately, it was not like my present handwriting, I wrote out a portion of it immediately under what I had written at your desire. You will thus observe, that while what I thus copied is identical in style with the sentences I had already written, it differs from the forged writing in many respects, which I will point out to you by and bye. The date of the entry of the diary to which I called your attention, brought before me a whole series of small circumstances, which reminded me of the devices by which Donato got possession of the two older papers; and you will remember, that in order to test the accuracy of my memory, I asked you to compare what I then wrote with the entry itself, unseen by me."

Bastiani was on the point of replying, when he was interrupted by a request from Evelyn that he would excuse the ladies from further attendance for the present.

"We are anxious," he said, "to deliver a packet which we have brought from Naples, and which ought to be forwarded without delay, and my friends have only just discovered that it is for a person in this very room. If they are not mistaken, they believe that the gentleman lying upon the sofa before us is the Cameriere Rinaldo, but so changed through illness that until now they had not recognised him."

As he spoke, Rinaldo rose, and leaning upon D'Urbino, came forward to meet Evelyn and the cousins.

"If the packet is from the Abate Noel," he said, speaking with difficulty, "it is for me."

Evelyn put the packet in his outstretched hand, while D'Urbino placed a chair for him, his agitation being so great that he would otherwise have sunk upon the floor.

His fingers trembled to such an extent that he could not untie the string which was around the parcel.

"Open it, D'Urbino," he said, "and read to me what it contains. It is for you as well as for me."

It contained a rather long letter from Noel, with a small enclosure. The letter was as follows:—

"Your friend was mistaken about the theft of the entry in the church register. I came upon it quite unexpectedly. The sacristan of one of the churches, whose registers I was examining, was murdered by one Lorenzo Galli, a brigand, who was guilty, by common report, of innumerable crimes. The sacristan was one of those sneaking rogues with whom the Neapolitan churches abound, and had played tricks with the registers of other parishes where he had been employed. His papers came into my hands; but they would have been profitless memoranda of past petty thefts, had it not been for the information I got from a poor country girl, Agnese Bruno, who had given her innocent heart to this doubly-dyed murderer Galli. How I first became acquainted with her Mr. Evelyn will tell you. The story is too long for a letter. The gist of the matter is, that her father had been a sort of partner-in-trade with this unhappy sacristan, and when it was discovered, as it was almost immediately, that her infamous lover was the murderer, she came to me in her misery, for such advice and help as I could give her. Galli, I should tell you, was found stabbed and dying in a wretched lodging in Naples; but before he died, he confessed the murder of the sacristan.

"Agnese Bruno, again, in the course of my inquiries about the past, mentioned the name D'Urbino more than once, her father having been a sort of hanger on to a family so called. I thought the name was familiar to me, and on recurring to your letter, I followed up the hints I thus gained from the girl. I found the missing registers in some out-of-the-way place where I should otherwise never have searched for them; and you now have, I believe, what your friend wished for. The entry is just what you led me to look for, and I send you a correct copy, duly authenticated. I should say that your friend who examined the register, and told you that it was mutilated, must have been misled by the condition of those of subsequent years, which have been shamefully kept, all kinds of people having been allowed free access to them."

As D'Urbino read this note aloud, all who were left in the room had gathered round Rinaldo, painfully interested by the intensity of the eagerness with which he was listening.

"Do I hear you right?" he asked with a bewildered look. "Does he say that the entry is there still, and that this wretch, Donato, has been practising upon my ignorant fears? Impossible! I was told by one of the truest of men, that Donato had been induced to let him examine the register and a portion of the stolen page together, and that the torn edges fitted into one another as exactly as if the page had been torn out before his eyes."

"But what of that, if the entry which you really sought for is still there uninjured?" asked D'Urbino. "Here is the copy, properly certified. It says that, on the twelfth of December, 1831, Bianca Gabrielli was married to Alessandro D'Urbino, in the church of Santa Maria dei Pellegrini, at Naples. Why, what is this?" he cried, turning to Rinaldo. "Who was Bianca Gabrielli? and what is she to you? This must be the record of my own father's second marriage, about which there was some mystery or other, and therefore it was never talked about when I was old enough to understand such things."

"Bianca Gabrielli," replied Rinaldo, taking D'Urbino's hand within his own, "was my sister and your mother, my dear boy."

"Impossible!" rejoined D'Urbino. "I was three years old at the date of this marriage with the Signorina Gabrielli."

Rinaldo dropped the hand that he held, and from the death-like pallor that overspread his face, the bystanders at first believed that death was to be the effect of the terrible blow that had shattered all his hopes. As he recovered and opened his eyes with a piteous longing for compassion, Giorgione, with an apology for putting himself forward, sat down before him and looked at him with a sad smile.

"Then you are Giovanni Gabrielli, and the brother of my dear wife, and none other."

Still gasping painfully for breath, Rinaldo hoarsely answered him: "I am Giovanni Rinaldo Gabrielli," he said; "but who in God's name are you? There is some dreadful delusion here."

"May I ask you, Colonel," said Giorgione, addressing Bastiani, "to allow me to look again at the fourth document that you just now showed me?"

Bastiani handed the paper to him, and Giorgione, turning over the first leaves, displayed a discoloured page of manuscript, lying loosely between the pages of the document that he held.

"This," he said, "is the page that your friend compared with the torn fragment remaining in the register; and among other entries this is one of them. It is the record of the marriage of Bianca D'Urbino, widow, with Filippo Giorgione, at the church of Santa Maria dei Pellegrini, on the 15th of May, in the year 1834. I am that Filippo Giorgione, and Francesca is her child and mine. She lived only three years, for her life was almost gone when she married me, through the atrocious calumnies and machinations of the diabolical villain whose last crime has been discovered this day."

Confounded by the startling intelligence, Rinaldo could not at once realise all its true importance. Then he put forth his arms, and leaning gently upon Francesca's shoulders, he steadily gazed into her beaming countenance, while one by one the tears dropped slowly from his eyes. She then flung herself into his arms, while he murmured, "Thank God! thank God! at last! at last!"

The bystanders meanwhile showed their sympathies and their gratification in their several characteristic ways. Margaret and Helen made no pretence at pretending not to cry. Evelyn looked at Margaret with a mightily affectionate smile, and said to himself, "By Jove! if D'Urbino does not fall in love with that girl, Francesca, he's more of a fool than I think him." Colonel Bastiani shook hands heartily with Giorgione, as Giorgione himself stood waiting to do the same with Rinaldo. D'Urbino's thoughts were exclusively with Francesca, but his heart was ready to melt with thankfulness at the recollection that Rinaldo's hopes were now no longer vain.

CHAPTER XI.

BIANCA GABRIELLI.

WHEN the first shock was over, the Colonel remembered that it was his duty to make further enquiries concerning the manner in which his prisoner, Donato, had been mixed up with the private affairs of so many persons. Having warmly congratulated Rinaldo on the result now attained, he asked how it was that Donato had contrived so completely to deceive him on a point apparently so easy to settle.

" And why, in Heaven's name," he added, " have you always gone among us as Rinaldo, and not as Gabrielli ? It seems to me that this change of name has been at the root of all the mischief that has happened."

"It must be a long story," replied Gabrielli, as he may now be called, "and I only know it very imperfectly myself. Giorgione here, my new friend and my sister's husband, knows far more about it than I do. But the reasons for my dropping my third name are easily told, and you will think, I trust, that I was right in what I did.

"You know that I am a Bolognese, and if you had passed any long time in Bologna some thirty or forty years ago, you would probably still remember that the mercantile house of which my father was the chief was then flourishing, so far as any house could flourish in the Bologna of those days. As soon as I was competent to the work, I was sent to Venice to negociate sundry business affairs with our correspondents there. These affairs were friendly in their character, but they occupied some years, during which I married a wife, intending before long to return to Bologna. And here, I should add, was the first beginning of my change of name There was another Gabrielli living in Venice, with whom I was in constant association, and by way of stopping the mistakes which arose from the confounding him and his affairs with me and my affairs, all our friends got into the habit of calling me by my two first names alone.

"Then came the first trouble. You know the Bolognesi are terrible Liberals, and so have been for generations and generations, and I was not less fierce in those days than other men of my own age. Shortly after my marriage I got into difficulties with the Austrian Government of Venice, which just then happened to be in a specially savage temper with its Italian subjects. The more they punished us, the fiercer were our denunciations; and the upshot was that before I had been two years married, I was consigned to the inside of an Austrian fortress, and there was I shut up for five miserable years. I was unhappy in having given personal offence to the governor of the fortress, and he treated me with all the cruelty in his power. He allowed me scarcely any communication with my wife and my friends, and for much more than half the time, I was shut out absolutely from the whole world outside the prison walls.

"When my term was completed, I returned to Venice a free man, only to find my wife and child dead, and the whole society in which I had mixed broken up and scattered, few people knew where. Lonely and despairing, I then left Venice for Bologna, as soon as the Venetian authorities would allow me to go. At Bologna, scarcely the wreck remained of all that I had loved. My father's mercantile house was gone to ruin, chiefly through the political troubles of the time; and he and my mother were both dead. My one sister, I was told, had married, but in another part of Italy, and it was believed that she too had died. All that I could learn with any certainty about her, was that D'Urbino was the name of the man who had married her, and that he was a Neapolitan. Another account given me was that she was not dead, but had become a nun, somewhere in the States of the Church, possibly in Rome itself.

"Then it was that I determined on continuing to adopt my second name as my surname. I was a marked man, stamped with the stigma of Austrian reprobation, and it was not likely that either the Roman or the Neapolitan governments would be willing to give either aid or employment to one who had been spending five years of his life in an Austrian prison. So I dropped the Gabrielli, and when afterwards I grew weary of the profitless search after my sister, associating from old habits with Liberals, but really caring little for politics, I applied for the post I now hold, I necessarily retained the name I had adopted. I asked for the office, not for its paltry salary, because I had contrived to get together enough from the wreck of our family fortunes to enable me to live, but because I hoped that it would bring me into contact with a large number of ecclesiastics, and would open to me the doors of many convents where as a marked Liberal I should be regarded with horror.

"I should tell you, too, that I had never been able to obtain a passport for the kingdom of Naples. Lists of all the people suspected by the Austrian police at Venice were kept at both the Neapolitan and Austrian embassies, and I was confident that the mere alteration of my name would not prevent my identification so long as I was connected with the Roman Liberal party.

"I need not trouble you with any account of the way I became acquainted with this miserable Donato. It was through a mere accident, and it was through another accident that I learnt from one of his accomplices in roguery, that in one of his drinking bouts he had been boasting that he had got hold of the register of a marriage between a Neapolitan D'Urbino and a lady who ran away from him and fled for refuge to a convent. When I came to sound the man himself about it, he soon suspected that I was interested in the stolen document, and he tempted me on and on, increasing his price, until it was impossible for me to meet it.

"When another chance made me acquainted with my dear D'Urbino here, and discovered that his family were Neapolitans, you will wonder why I did not at once put to him the questions I so longed to ask. I will tell you why I did not; and if you knew by experience what it is to be alone in the world, desolate, with no one to love, and no one to suffer for, you would forgive the error, if error it really was.

"In the first place, he belonged to the political party which regarded me as a renegade, and moreover as a hired spy. Had I gone straight to him, he would have repudiated all connection with me for ever. Nor had I any trustworthy grounds for believing that he was, what I began to suspect, my own sister's son. Nor again had I any real knowledge of his own personal character. To have found him, the only human being in the world that belonged to me, and to whom I belonged, a graceless, unprincipled, selfish scamp, would have broken my heart; therefore, until I could satisfy myself as to his habits of life and principles, and had conquered the personal aversion which I saw that he was disposed to feel towards me, I resolved to keep my own counsel; and with no little difficulty I kept it almost to the last."

"Yes, Cameriere," said Colonel Bastiani,

as Gabrielli ended his story, given as it had been with many pauses for the sake of rest, and amidst many expressions of sympathy and requests for clearer explanations from his hearers, "it seems a very natural and common-place proceeding altogether. I don't see how you could have done otherwise. Your case is one of hundreds. You have always seemed to me a devilish odd sort of a fellow to belong to the Papal household, but I can't make out that you have not as good a right to be there as half the men that swarm in the Vatican. I had hoped, at the same time, that you would have more to tell about this scoundrel below stairs. If you are right in suspecting that he stole the church register, he is guilty of what they call sacrilege, and you know what that means in the clerical government under which I have the small honour to serve. The fellow must be an uncommonly clever scamp besides."

"There you are undoubtedly right, Colonel," interposed Giorgione, "though he is only a common-place blackguard, both in his passions and his crimes. Whether he has any struggling remains of conscience in him, I will not pretend to say, but ever since I have known him, his history has been that of a revengeful, dissipated, needy, unscrupulous, and sneaking scoundrel.

"When I first became intimate with the Gabrielli household at Bologna, which was some time after our friend the Cameriere had gone to Venice, this Donato was beginning to cause them great annoyance through his pretensions to the Signorina Bianca. He held some office in the municipality which brought him a good deal into contact with them, and he was understood to come of a wealthy family, as he certainly was a well-educated man. At that time I was engaged in some scientific enquiries, hoping to be nominated to a professorship in the university there, as my father had given up all hope of seeing me, with my bookish tastes, succeed him in his banking affairs. With a rare kindness, indeed, he reconciled himself to my caprices, and it was understood that, banker or no banker, I was to be well provided for.

"As by degrees my intimacy with the Gabriellis increased, Donato began to impute Signorina Bianca's persistent refusals of his hand to a preference for myself; and accordingly he laid a scheme for separating us, and for forcing the Signorina to accept him as her husband. It was the same scheme that has been practised and has succeeded hundreds of times before, but if it had been practised thousands instead of hundreds of times, it would have been none the less cowardly and diabolical.

"You know, as we all know too well, how easy it is to destroy the friendship of us Italians by plausible lyings of the most trumpery nature. This was Donato's first move. Before the summer was out in which he began to backbite, and insinuate, and to act the candid friend of both houses, the Gabriellis and the Giorgiones had learnt to hate one another with all the hatred that this wretched man could desire. The marriage between the Signorina and myself, which was already in contemplation, was forbidden by the parents on both sides; and my father contrived to have me sent off to South America on a botanical expedition, to put an end to all possibility of a clandestine marriage.

"Before this, however, this wretched plotter had made his second move. By various devices he contrived to convince Signorina Bianca's father that she was carrying on a secret correspondence with myself. Next, he played some devilish trick which persuaded the infuriated Gabrielli that his daughter was actually in the habit of meeting me alone in the summer evenings. At last, he worked the unhappy father up to such a pitch of frenzy, by the reports he brought him, that he swore that she should either enter a convent or agree to take Donato as her husband. He had all along been less averse to the man than the Signorina and her mother, being deceived by his plausible address and the reputation of his family for wealth.

"When the alternative was offered to the Signorina, she chose the convent without an instant's hesitation, only stipulating that before any step was taken, she should visit an old relation of her mother's, who was the superioress of a Benedictine convent near Naples. To this friendly nun she unfolded all her griefs. The nun proved to be a very kind-hearted old lady, and she amazed the Signorina by proposing a third alternative. She was the sweetest, the pleasantest, and the prettiest old lady I could conceive; and in after years, when my heart was broken, I often went to the dreary-looking convent, and came away from its little parlour, I will not say comforted, but strengthened to live and act like a Christian man, for the sake of my little Francesca. Alas! alas! the dear woman died while Francesca was still a little child!

"This was her scheme. She took into her confidence your own father, my dear D'Urbino, who often visited the convent to see some relation who was a nun there. Your father was then an old man, in enfeebled health, and still mourning for your mother, who had been dead about two years. What these ladies and gentlemen, especially Signor Evelyn, and the two English ladies, will say to the proposal which this romantic old nun made to Signor D'Urbino, I cannot guess. She proposed to him that he should marry the Signorina Bianca, and thus give her the status of a married woman, arranging that immediately after the wedding the bride should return to the Convent, and there reside.

"To all this, he, like the noble man that he was, at once agreed, provided, of course, that Gabrielli the elder would give his consent. That consent was not withheld, and the marriage took place. The newly-made Signora D'Urbino returned to the convent, and hence the story about her having quarrelled with your father and fled to a nunnery. He died a year or two afterwards, and the widow remained with the old superioress as before."

"But how about this Donato?" interrupted the Colonel, who had with difficulty concealed the impatience with which he had listened to all these details of Giorgione's private affairs. "I want to get at his motives, and at some proof of his theft of the marriage register."

"It is to that I am now coming," replied Giorgione, "and you will pardon me if I have wearied you with my personal history and past sorrows. When I came back from America, I found that the same panic which had brought the house of Gabrielli to the ground, had broken up my own father's prosperity, and he barely lived to give me an account of all that had happened. After his death I cared for nothing, and life was almost a blank before me, absence having only intensified my love for her of whom I could not bear to speak as the Signora D'Urbino. From my father, however, I learnt where she was living, and through a third person I communicated with her friend the superioress of the convent.

"On what followed, I need not dwell. A year after Signor D'Urbino's death, I married his bride widow, and once more life seemed worth living for; then again that miserable man reappeared, to be the curse of my days. He had gone down in the world, as men like him do go down, and was living by his wits, which means he was picking up a precarious existence by trading upon the fears, the hopes, the follies and the crimes of others. I was living then at Pisa, where I was not a marked man as I was at Bologna, and where there were no painful memories to darken our happiness, struggling to obtain a scientific professorship in the university. Whether or not Donato came to Pisa by chance, or with the deliberate intention of annoying us for the purpose of extorting money, I know not.

"As soon as he did find us out, he told me distinctly that he would spread reports in the city, which would inevitably injure me through injuring the reputation of my wife, unless I paid him for his silence. I defied him, conscious that I had only to bring forward the history of the D'Urbino marriage to blast him as a maligner, and to drive him from the place in shame. After this, we heard no more of him for some time. Then he again presented himself with a horrid look of triumph in his face. The hour for his revenge upon me and my wife was come, he said, and unless the sum of money that he named was paid to him, he would inform the rector of the university that I was an impostor, that the story of my having legally married the widow of D'Urbino was a fabrication; that in reality I had carried her off from the convent, where she had become a nun, and had married her in Switzerland.

"Again I defied him, when he produced the leaf that he had stolen from the church register, and fled from my presence as I sprang forwards to snatch it from his hands. What, I ask you, could I do in the meshes of such a net, spread by such a miscreant? It was the old story over again;—incessant threats, and payments of such miserable sums as he could wring from my poverty. The amount he demanded for the possession of the stolen register was beyond my utmost resources, and I could only stave off his slanders by occasional payments. It was useless to denounce him before any magistrate, for he would instantly have destroyed the paper, and with it all proof of his own guilt and of the truth of any statements concerning myself.

"Under this persecution my wife sickened and died, a year after the birth of Francesca. With Francesca I then left Pisa, a broken-down man. After many wanderings, always an object of suspicion on account of my political sympathies, we finally settled in this very house, hoping in the crowd to escape the tortures inflicted by our persecutor. I found that I could just live in a humble way by the art I had once learnt for my pleasure only, and I was comparatively at peace, when the wretched man again came upon the scene, and finding me engaged in a profitable occupation, recommenced the old extortions.

"What would be the effect of a mere hint to the Roman police, that I had carried off an Italian nun and married her in a Protestant country, I need not tell you. And without any marriage certificate, how was I to prove the true facts of the case? Knowing this, too, you will not wonder that I never acquainted young D'Urbino with the connection that existed between his family and myself. Liberal as he might be in all his notions, I felt assured that in the present state of Italian society, he would resent the running away with his father's cloistered widow as a scandalous outrage. No register proved my legal marriage, and after the lapse of more than twenty years, the present inmates of the convent would retain no traditions of a supposed event, which at the time that it was supposed to have happened, would have been sedulously hushed up.

"How Donato came to commit the blunder of leaving the stolen leaf among the papers he concealed here, is now clear enough. These ladies frightened him out of his senses, for he is as cowardly as he is villainous, and in his haste he heaped the whole contents of his pockets into the opening. And I should explain his unexpected return by his having discovered the mistake he had made."

"Then now my course is clear," said Colonel Bastiani, as Giorgione ended his narrative. "I must arrest you on the double charge of having in your possession treasonable papers and the stolen register. I will leave you in your own house, nevertheless, in charge of three of my men, and I will endeavour to obtain the consent of the Governor of Rome for your liberation, on the personal undertaking of Cameriere Rinaldo Gabrielli, which he will doubtless give, that you remain in Rome until called up for trial, and for the purpose of giving evidence against this ruffian Donato, whom I shall now carry with me and lodge safely in prison."

With this Colonel Bastiani took his leave, and left the wondering kinsfolk and their friends to realise the unalloyed enjoyment and happiness to which not one of them had looked forward when the morning of the day had dawned.

CHAPTER XII.

FOR THE WEARY, REST.

"I ALWAYS thought that Giorgione—by the way, I suppose he is to be Signor Giorgione now—was a strangely cultivated person for a man engaged in a mere mechanical trade," observed Margaret, as in company with her cousin and Evelyn, she left the house of the mosaic-worker for that of her aunt, shortly after the departure of Bastiani.

"And a most dignified personage into the bargain," replied Helen. "What say you to his manner, Mr. Evelyn?"

"As to his manners and accomplishments," rejoined Evelyn, "at the present moment I am absolutely disinclined to discuss them. My mind is wholly occupied by two important questions: — Is D'Urbino going to marry the charming Francesca? and how can we ensure ourselves some dinner by the shortest possible process? Somebody says '*La joie fait peur ;*' but if our worthy neighbour's sensations just now are at all like mine, they must be crying out '*La joie fait faim*' with a vengeance."

Helen indulged in a smile so peculiar, that Evelyn concluded that she knew more on the first of his questions than she chose to avow. Margaret more practically answered his second question.

"I suppose that it is just possible that you might dine with us," she said, "and that a tolerable dinner may be ordered from a *trattoria*."

"But what will the prudishness and priggishness of aristocratic Rome say to such a proceeding?" asked Evelyn, with pretended gravity.

"We will reply that I was here to act as the most unimpeachable of duennas," said Helen.

"Suppose we get over the difficulty by asking the excellent D'Urbino to join us," replied Evelyn. "He has lost an expected uncle, but that is no reason why he should not find an unexpected dinner. And then I will pump him as to the fair Francesca. Nobody drinks toasts in Rome, or else we would drink success to everybody, including ourselves, so often that—you understand Latin, I know, Miss Sandford—*in vino veritas*,—before the evening was over he should confide all his hopes and fears to my sympathetic bosom."

As he spoke, the door of the room where they had seated themselves was thrown open, and the old woman who was in charge of the house, announced Signor D'Urbino.

"*Diavolo! Diavolo! Diavolo!*" exclaimed Evelyn.

Without heeding this somewhat singular

greeting, D'Urbino proceeded to say that he had thought it better to leave the uncle and the newly found niece, and her father, to themselves, and could not go home without offering his hearty thanks for what Evelyn and the cousins had done in answer to his letter.

"My dear fellow," interrupted Evelyn, "thanks at the present moment are as entirely *de trop* as you would have been if you had stayed with the enraptured two next door. Just now everything is *mal à propos*, except the ordering of dinner. We had just arranged, first to order dinner somewhere, and secondly to ask you to come and share the humble meal with us. If you are as hungry as I am, you must have the appetite of an accepted lover."

The moment he had uttered the words, which he had intended for a clever *ruse* for calling up a traitorous glow upon D'Urbino's cheeks, he perceived that they were in truth a confession of the happy position in which he was himself placed with regard to Margaret.

"Am I really to wish you joy, then?" asked D'Urbino, with a cordial smile that threw all Evelyn's calculations into confusion.

"My dear D'Urbino," he answered, "you were born expressly by a mistake of nature to make me look foolish. Take my advice, and never ask a man to explain the similitudes with which he adorns his conversation. The practical question is, dinner—how? and where?"

"I am about to make a bold proposal," returned D'Urbino. "Miss Osborne mentioned one day that she should like to know how a *bonâ fide* inhabitant of Rome like myself dined, when served, or tyrannised over, by an old woman like my unpleasant Betta. Some sort of materials for dinner she must certainly have prepared for Signore Rinaldo and myself. Will you all come in an hour's time, and see what she and I together can prepare for you in the purely Italian way of cookery."

"Do say yes," Helen whispered to Margaret, who looked inquiringly at Evelyn, who looked in return at D'Urbino, who without hesitation answered his own question. "In an hour, then, we shall expect you." And away he strode, humming a merry tune.

A little more than an hour afterwards all the four were seated round a table in the studio in the Via Felice. The bed which Gabrielli had so lately occupied was banished and the room was all in order, Francesca's portrait seeming to preside as a tutelary genius over the assembled guests and their host.

"One barbarism you must be pleased to condone, Miss Sandford," observed D'Urbino, as they seated themselves. "It is not our habit to crowd a whole dinner on the table at once, but my housekeeper's feelings were so fluttered as well as flattered by the honour you are doing her, that if I had entrusted any portion of the cooking to her undirected energies, it would assuredly have come to grief. She is now reposing on her laurels in the kitchen."

"What a blessing it is to be able to cook!" remarked Evelyn, with a sigh of envy. "All this feast has been prepared and served in less than an hour's time! wonderful indeed! soup! sausage! no doubt from Bologna! eggs! omelette! cutlets! no doubt of veal! salad! oranges! figs! Yes, in the name of the prophet, figs! Why, D'Urbino, if you never did a good action in your life before, you did a good deed to-day when you asked us to dine with you. And now, my good friend, pray let us leave off talking, that you may ask us to begin without delay."

"I am delighted to see you so happy!" rejoined D'Urbino, as he began distributing the soup, satisfied in his own mind that all this effervescence was the consequence of his friend's success in his suit with Margaret.

As the dinner began, so it proceeded, and so it ended. When it was over, Margaret asked whether the old Betta would be affronted if they asked her to show them over her kitchen arrangements and to enlighten them on the secrets of Roman cookery and management. The old woman proved most complaisant, and Evelyn was left alone with his host.

"When is it to be, Evelyn?" D'Urbino said to him, as if asking the simplest commonplace question.

"When is what to be?" asked Evelyn, pretending to be in the dark.

"Surely you meant your similitude, as you called it, to be an intimation of your happiness."

"I certainly did not mean it to be so," said Evelyn, "but there is really no reason for concealment;" and he told him all.

Then the crafty man began to ponder in his own mind how best to extract from D'Urbino the information which he desired.

But he could not fix his thoughts steadily upon any topic that might lead naturally to the subject he wished to introduce, and he gradually grew silent and thoughtful. D'Urbino, too, seemed indisposed for much talk. By degrees Evelyn resolved to dismiss the question from his mind, and yielded to the graver thoughts that were stealing over him.

"A wonderful man is this friend of yours," he observed, as D'Urbino still sat silent and meditating; "and what a life to have lived."

"He has but little life remaining before him," replied D'Urbino. "To me it seems that death is in every look of his countenance. I should rejoice to know how best I could sweeten the few days he will still be with us."

Evelyn made no reply, and they relapsed again into silence.

"Evelyn, my friend," at length D'Urbino began, "you shall decide for me what I shall do. I intend to ask Francesca Giorgione to be my wife, and I have reason to believe that she will not say 'no.' But I am in the greatest perplexity to decide whether to postpone the question in the expectation that Gabrielli might possibly so far recover, as to be in a less agitated and exhausted state than he now is; or to ask it without delay, expecting that his last hours cannot be far off, and knowing that he would rejoice to learn that the marriage was arranged before he left us."

"It is a difficult question," Evelyn answered, as soon as he could recover from his surprise; "a most difficult question. On the whole, had you not better hear what his doctor says about his probable recovery, before deciding?"

"The doctor has told me again and again," rejoined D'Urbino, "that his system is utterly worn out, and that he cannot possibly survive another serious shock of it."

"Then," said Evelyn, "speak to the young lady and her father without a day's delay."

Nothing more passed between them, and each was still deep in his own thoughts, when the cousins came in to claim Evelyn as their escort home. D'Urbino walked with them to Mrs. Sandford's door, and there they parted, Evelyn to his hotel, and D'Urbino to his own home, after calling to learn how Gabrielli had borne the excitements of the day. It would have been impossible to remove him, even if a removal had been thought of for a moment, under the circumstances in which they all found themselves. The tidings that D'Urbino received served only to confirm him in his resolution to act upon Evelyn's advice.

As early as propriety would allow, he was there again on the following morning, and had no difficulty in obtaining a private interview with Francesca.

"Francesca, my love," he began, with a

suddenness that put to flight the small amount of self-possession which she had summoned up; "we have one duty now before us."

A thrill of happiness at hearing him thus identify his actions with her own, restored to her some degree of self-control.

"It is our first duty," he continued, "to brighten the last days of your uncle Gabrielli, now that the hopes of so many years are fulfilled at last."

"Oh! signore!" she cried in terror, "what is it that you mean? He is not going to die. Tell me anything but that."

"There is time just now for nothing but our duties towards *him*," he replied; "but, Francesca, it is not to be 'Signore' any more towards me."

Her heart throbbed violently, but the torrent of delight that his words created was controlled by the old habit of reverencing him as too great and too noble for anything but silent admiration.

"He will not die," she said, "he cannot die now. It is not the will of God. He will live now, because he is happy at last."

"He will be still happier soon," replied D'Urbino, in the same hopeless voice, "but we shall not be with him. Oh! Francesca, it is hard to tell you this, now that you are losing him as soon as you have found him; and neither you, nor any living being but myself, know all the greatness and goodness of this wonderful man. You shall hear it all some day. This much I must say now, that he will be happier if he knows that you and I may attend him to the last, pledged to each other to be man and wife before the coming spring is over. May I go and speak to your father, my child? If you mean 'yes,' say nothing, and I shall understand your unspoken love."

She said nothing, but timidly put out her hand, without looking him in the face. The tenderness and respectfulness with which he lightly kissed it, first helped her to realise the equality of the position to which he had already raised her with himself, and when he was gone, she still did not raise her eyes from the ground, but went on murmuring, " It seems impossible ! it seems impossible !"

Giorgione received the lover's request with but little surprise. It seemed to him a natural arrangement, and in the uncertainty of his own relations towards the government, he confessed that he should have a mind far more at ease if Francesca were happy in the protection of a good and honourable husband. He told D'Urbino that he had long ago satisfied himself that he was not an unworthy son of a father to whom, for the sake of Francesca's mother, he was under such profound obligations; and that had it been otherwise, he and Francesca would never have been acquainted. "The seal of death, too," he said, " is upon that sweet and sorrowful countenance, and it is well that you have done this. I will go and prepare him myself, and when I send, bring Francesca with you to his bedside."

When they were summoned, they found Giorgione standing at the foot of the bed, and cautioning them by his gestures to avoid the display of any exciting emotion. D'Urbino led Francesca forward.

Gabrielli was too weak to speak aloud, and Francesca stooped to hear what he wished to say to her. He slowly lifted up his thin, worn hand, and stroked her hair and forehead.

"*Francesca mia!*" he then said, feebly, "I have loved you ever since the day when I first saw you by the fountain in the moonlight."

She ventured, as she thought, almost too boldly, to kiss his brow, and then stood aside. From the movement of his eyes, D'Urbino then saw that Gabrielli wished to speak to him, and he bent his head downwards.

"*Fioravante mio!*" said Gabrielli, in the same low tones, "God bless you!" Then, after a pause, "and her too."

At a sign from Giorgione, the two then left the room. When Francesca had a little recovered herself, they sat down to talk.

"*Signore!*" she began.

D'Urbino smiled and shook his head.

"*Caro Signore!*" she corrected herself.

He shook his head again.

"*Caro mio!*" she resumed, with a little hesitation.

"Well, *Carissima*," he said, "for the present that will do; and what were you going to say?"

"He is not going to die," she replied.

"God grant it!" he said; "but what can possibly make you think so, Francesca?"

"I have seen three persons die," she answered, "and he does not look as they looked."

Her father shortly afterwards came in with the intelligence that Gabrielli was none the worse for the news he had heard, and that Francesca was to sit by his side until he woke from the slumber into which he seemed falling. D'Urbino went with her to the chamber door, and before it was reached he had slipped a ring upon one of her willing fingers, loving her all the more for the innocent coyness and shyness with which she accepted every fresh mark of his affection.

"Oh! *mio caro!*" she said, "what is this?"

"Is it *caro* still, or *carissimo?*" he asked, with a pretended frown.

She hung down her head, and he could just hear the whispered "*carissimo*," as she passed into the sick man's chamber.

Gabrielli was already asleep, and Francesca sat by his side, herself dreaming waking dreams, and totally unconscious of the flight of the rosy hours. Could it be really her own hand, she thought, on which she saw the pretty trinket, and from which she never lifted her eyes, except now and then to watch the quiet sleep of the slumberer? It was long past noonday when she noted a change in his appearance. Young as she was, she was already familiar with the signs of the sick bed.

"It is certainly true!" she said to herself. "It cannot be the sunlight only! There is more colour in his cheeks than there was before! He is going to wake! Oh, my God! if it please thee! if it please thee!"

Soon Gabrielli opened his eyes. He was not at all astonished at seeing her by his side, but she was speedily convinced that he was better, for he put to her the very common-place question of healthy sleepers, "Have I been long asleep?"

"Two or three hours only," she replied.

"What is that I see upon your finger, *carissima?*" he asked her after a pause, and in a firmer tone of voice.

She held her hand nearer to him, to show him the sparkling gem. "He gave it to me to-day," she said.

Then with an amused smile, he patted

the outstretched fingers, saying as he did it, "*Bella! Bella!*"

A sudden impulse of harmless coquetry came over the delighted girl, and she mischievously replied, "Which is pretty? the ring, or the hand?"

"We will ask *him* that question, *carina*," he replied.

Again a pause, followed by another common-place question, most consoling to her heart.

"Francesca, what o'clock is it?"

She told him the hour.

"Do you know that I am rather hungry?" he said; "I am an old man, and cannot support nature by looking at lover's gifts."

She was on her feet in an instant, and could scarcely refrain from clapping her hands with joy at these signs of returning strength.

"Do you mind my leaving you for five minutes?" she asked him.

Receiving the permission she expected, she left the room, and quickly closing the door, flew down stairs, and rushed fairly into the arms of Margaret and Helen before she was aware of their presence. They were waiting for her uncle's waking, to learn what report there might be as to the possibility of his recovery. Her beaming eyes rendered all enquiries needless.

"What ought he to have?" she exclaimed. "Oh, Signorina, pray tell me! you know it so much better than I do!"

"Is the child out of her senses?" returned Helen, taken aback by the incomprehensible query.

"Oh, pray forgive me!" she hurriedly returned; "I really am out of my senses. He is better, and he is not going to die, and I am so happy at last!"

"How can you tell this, my dear Francesca?" said Margaret, distrusting Francesca's diagnosis altogether.

"But are people ever hungry when they

are going to die?" rejoined Francesca, with an exquisite mixture of simplicity and sadness, which so tickled the fancy of Evelyn, who just then followed the cousins into the room, that he found it impossible to resist his impulse to reply himself to the question.

"Certainly not," he exclaimed, with all the dogmatic positiveness that he could assume. "Signorina Giorgione," he continued, "you are one of the most sensible young ladies with whom I was ever acquainted, and I foresee that it is decreed by my destiny that we should become fast friends."

Fortunately at this point the discussion was put an end to by the entrance of the doctor. His report was entirely favourable. He saved his own reputation as a medical prophet by reminding those who cared to listen, that it was not a shock of pleasure and excitement which he had dreaded for his patient, but only a shock of sorrow;

and Francesca, radiant with happiness, but profoundly indifferent to the doctor's consistency, returned to her uncle's bedside with a supply of coffee, bread, and fruit.

"Well," observed Helen, as she and her cousin with Evelyn left the house, and turned in the direction of the Pincio, "what say you to the doctor and his prognostics?"

"I say nothing at all to the doctor," Evelyn replied; "but I say this, that if that fellow D'Urbino is led away by most unsound views on the subject of revolutions, his taste in rings is altogether unexceptionable."

"What can you possibly know about his taste in rings?" asked Margaret. "Has he been consulting you? or is it you that have been consulting him?"

"Margaret has a fair complexion, remember, Mr. Evelyn," interposed Helen, with a glance full of meaning.

"And the beautiful Francesca is unquestionably a brunette," retorted Evelyn.

"Do you mean that Signor D'Urbino has been really consulting you about the kind of jewellery most suited to Francesca's complexion?" asked Helen.

"It is really gratifying to me, Miss Sandford," he rejoined, "it is quite consolatory, indeed, to find that two young women can be in the same room with another young woman, and not discover that she is wearing a pretty trinket, quite new. But, as I said before, D'Urbino's taste in rings deserves my warmest commendation, and I shall devote a serious study to the ascertaining what will be the most becoming ornament for me to offer to the bride."

"Charles, you are jesting with us," Margaret remonstrated. "Is he really thinking of marrying Francesca? And how could you possibly have found it out?"

"He told me yesterday that he was going to ask her to marry him——"

"And you never told us," interrupted Margaret. "That is really too bad."

" Because he told me of his own accord, and desired me to tell no one till all was settled," he replied.

" And has he told you to-day that it *is* settled ?" asked Margaret.

" By no means," he said; "the ring on Francesca's finger told me that."

" Who would have conceived that you, of all men in the world, should be chosen by Signor D'Urbino to be the recipient of his love confidences ?" exclaimed Helen, now fairly astonished.

" Miss Sandford," he rejoined, " you have no conception of the amount of latent sentimentalism in my character."

" *De non apparentibus et non existentibus,*" Helen began, carrying on the jest, " *eadem——*"

" My dear Margaret," cried Evelyn, "your cousin's accomplishments are more than I can bear. Latin again, and not only Latin, but law Latin. Thank heaven ! here comes the *innamorato* himself. You two shall walk on, and I will lay hold of him and follow in your wake."

It was useless to resist, and Margaret and Helen obeyed.

"I wish you joy, my dear fellow," said Evelyn, "with all my heart. She looks splendid this morning, and the ring is infinitely becoming. There now! don't put on that absurd countenance. I saw it on her hand, as she rushed down stairs to say that the fine old fellow—Mephistopheles the Good, you know—was better, and was shouting for his dinner on the top of the stairs."

"You would not talk all this nonsense, Evelyn," rejoined D'Urbino, "unless there was reason in it. For God's sake, tell me the truth and nothing else."

"The doctor came while we were there, and confessed that he thought his patient would recover. And now we will overtake those others, and say good-bye, before we start for Naples."

A few strides brought them together, and they stood beneath the leafless trees on the ever-pleasant Pincian slopes.

"You may congratulate him without fear, Margaret," said Evelyn. "I have exhausted all my efforts to induce him to announce his happiness himself, but the incurable modesty and timidity of his character are more than can be overcome."

The congratulations were quickly made, and as quickly returned. They were on the point of parting, when Evelyn, in a half-whisper, observed to D'Urbino, "I admire your notions about rings. Have you any views on necklaces, or are they an abomination in your eyes? Of course you hate ear-rings, or you would not have chosen *Francesca la bella.*"

"I think I have observed, that Miss Osborne wears ear-rings," said D'Urbino, resolved on one return shot, at the least.

"Don't speak of it, as you love me," returned Evelyn, in pretended distress. "Between ourselves, her education has been sadly neglected in that respect."

"What is that you are saying, Signor D'Urbino?" interposed Margaret, who had caught a few words of the dialogue.

"He says that he cannot endure ear-rings," replied Evelyn, looking as mischievous as he could.

"Pardon me, Miss Osborne," exclaimed D'Urbino; "I never uttered a word on the subject of my likes or dislikes. Evelyn himself argued that I could not like ear-rings because I admired Francesca. But I confess I don't see the force of the reasoning."

"Not see it?" cried Evelyn. "It's as clear as the day. The Signorina Giorgione is very handsome. Therefore whoever admires her must have good taste. Signor D'Urbino admires her, therefore he has good taste, or in other words, he does not like ear-rings."

"Now, Mr. Evelyn," exclaimed Helen,

laughing, "you are hoist with your own petard."

"Shakspeare!" observed Evelyn, with a bow.

"You laugh at my Latin," Helen continued, undisturbed; "now note your own logic. Whoever likes ear-rings has bad taste. Miss Osborne likes ear-rings, therefore she has bad taste. But Mr. Evelyn admires Miss Osborne, therefore he admires a person who has bad taste, and therefore he has bad taste himself. Now confess, Mr. Evelyn, is not my logic as good as yours?"

"My dear Miss Sandford," rejoined Evelyn, "you will make us lose the train, if you continue talking any longer. Believe me, it is too cold to argue out-of-doors in February."

"Incorrigible as ever!" said Helen to D'Urbino, as at length they parted.

The trees on the Pincio had burst into

their full leaf in all the brilliant effulgence of an Italian spring, when the four friends strolled along its slopes once more, about to find the fulfilment of the hopes with which they had parted on the calm February afternoon. But their whole party was nearly doubled in number, and not the least lively of them all was Gabrielli himself, now so far recovered as to enjoy the fresh April breezes.

"Miss Osborne, my dear," he was saying to Margaret, as she sat down on a bench by his side; — (he had got into a pleasant, fatherly sort of way of thus addressing Margaret and her cousin)—" our friend Evelyn is developing in me a faculty which I hardly knew to exist. I have laughed more during the last two or three weeks than I have laughed in my whole life before. He will be a good husband to you, my dear. And he has shown me the necklace that he is to give to Francesca to-morrow."

"He told me he should show it to you," Margaret replied. "He said that he felt just like a big school-girl, unable to keep her own secrets."

"It is superb," said Gabrielli; "it is too superb for my Francesca, who, you know, will not be the wife of a rich man."

"It will not be too handsome for the neck that is to carry it," said Margaret. "What a beautiful neck it is, too!"

"Do you know, my dear," he went on, "that I believe that Francesca has no idea of her own beauty."

"She is the most humble, unaffected girl I ever met with, in Italy or out of it," said Margaret, with undisguised warmth of admiration.

"Thank you, my dear, for saying so," he replied. "Thank you with all my heart. I think so myself, but it is pleasant to hear the same from another, and from you too. I am very glad to find that D'Urbino sees that charm in her character, and has the wisdom to value that greatest of all virtues."

"Cameriere!" exclaimed Evelyn, coming up and interrupting them, "we are puzzled as to what you were doing this morning, for so many hours, in D'Urbino's studio. Are you to appear shortly as the central figure of a colossal group in marble?" As Gabrielli seemed a little confused at the question, Margaret came to his help, repeating what he had said about the development of his capacity for laughter under Evelyn's guidance.

"As far as I can make out, Margaret," retorted Evelyn, "Signor Gabrielli seems to be developing a capacity for flirting, under another accomplished teacher."

"Ah! my dear! my dear!" said the Cameriere, with a smile, turning to Margaret as they rose to return home. "Let him have his laugh while he is young, and can make others laugh also. Let him say what he will, you shall let me lean on your arm as we go down this little hill. It is to be the last day, you know."

"Until you pay us the promised visit in England," rejoined Evelyn, offering him an arm on the other side.

The double wedding was on the following day. No one beyond the families of the brides and bridesgrooms was present, saving only the still disconsolate Della Porta, who, however, bore himself cheerfully, and was of vast use in paying such attentions to Mrs. Sandford as duty and propriety required. Early in the morning two small, polished, oak boxes arrived at Mrs. Sandford's house, addressed to Margaret. She read the letter that accompanied them, handing to Helen the keys which it contained, that she might open them and gratify her wondering curiosity.

"This one first with the inlaid mosaic on the top," she cried. "Why, Margaret, it is the dear old Cameriere himself! What a charming little bust, and what exquisite marble! Oh! what a delightful present! And what can be in the other, I wonder?"

"That box that you have opened is for Charles," replied Margaret, "but the letter says that I was to open it. The other is for me."

"It's Charles Evelyn himself!" exclaimed Helen, delighted. "Certainly one may trust an Italian to do the kindest thing in the most graceful way. And this accounts, no doubt, for the late mysterious closetings with our gallant Cavaliere. The mosaic, I suppose, is a pretty little attention from Francesca's father."

"I hope you will be as happy some day yourself, dearest," said Helen, kissing her cousin with a long embrace, and not trusting herself to say more.

When the weddings were over, Margaret found time to say hurriedly to D'Urbino:—

"You could not possibly have given us anything that we should treasure more. And don't let Francesca forget to bring the arm as we go down this little hill. It is to be the last day, you know."

"Until you pay us the promised visit in England," rejoined Evelyn, offering him an arm on the other side.

The double wedding was on the following day. No one beyond the families of the brides and bridesgrooms was present, saving only the still disconsolate Della Porta, who, however, bore himself cheerfully, and was of vast use in paying such attentions to Mrs. Sandford as duty and propriety required. Early in the morning two small, polished, oak boxes arrived at Mrs. Sandford's house, addressed to Margaret. She read the letter that accompanied them, handing to Helen the keys which it contained, that she might open them and gratify her wondering curiosity.

"This one first with the inlaid mosaic on the top," she cried. "Why, Margaret, it is the dear old Cameriere himself! What a charming little bust, and what exquisite marble! Oh! what a delightful present! And what can be in the other, I wonder?"

"That box that you have opened is for Charles," replied Margaret, "but the letter says that I was to open it. The other is for me."

"It's Charles Evelyn himself!" exclaimed Helen, delighted. "Certainly one may trust an Italian to do the kindest thing in the most graceful way. And this accounts, no doubt, for the late mysterious closetings with our gallant Cavaliere. The mosaic, I suppose, is a pretty little attention from Francesca's father."

"I hope you will be as happy some day yourself, dearest," said Helen, kissing her cousin with a long embrace, and not trusting herself to say more.

When the weddings were over, Margaret found time to say hurriedly to D'Urbino:—

"You could not possibly have given us anything that we should treasure more. And don't let Francesca forget to bring the necklace, when you come to see us in England."

"God bless you for all your goodness to her," he said, wringing her hand.

Another equally short dialogue passed between two others of the assembled party.

"Have I any chance yet, Miss Sandford?" said the Marchese to Helen, as soon as it was possible to speak without being heard by any third person.

"Not yet," she replied, readily, as if prepared for the question.

"May I ask again in a year's time?" he said.

"If you wish it," she replied.

At the end of the year, he did ask her again; but she shook her head.

"May I ask once more at the end of another year?" he said with a touching patience.

"It will be too soon," she answered.

But he did ask her, when the second twelve-month was over; and remembering his gallant feat in stopping the runaway horse on the road to Pompeii, she accepted him.

Six months after they were married, Helen received a cordial letter of congratulation from Henry Noel, dated from Sydney, where he was settled as a University Professor. It further contained a message for Gabrielli :—" If you have an opportunity of seeing the Cameriere," it said, "tell him that I am hard at work and happy, and have practically learnt the truth of the saying that '*Labor improbus omnia vincit.*'"

When the Cameriere received the letter which Helen sent on to him without delay, he saw in a moment that by the underscoring of the word "omnia," more was meant than the author of the famous saying ever dreamed of.

"Yes," he murmured to himself, "*Laborare est orare. Deo gratias!*"

As for the miserable traitor Donato, his career of cruel treachery and savage selfishness was finally closed on the day when he was arrested at the moment of his expected triumph. There was no need for any fresh trial on any new charges against him. The sentence of death still hung over his head, and but for the earnest intercession of Gabrielli himself, he would have been hanged before the week was over. As it was, he was sentenced to imprisonment for life— a fate which the regulations of the Roman prisons speedily converted into a capital punishment, for before spring had come, he was laid low with the gaol-fever, and died.

Upon Francesca's marriage, Gabrielli and Giorgione, the latter of whom had been liberated within four-and-twenty hours of his arrest, to her surprise and trouble, steadfastly refused to become inmates of the D'Urbino household.

"We shall be infinitely better friends, *carina*, if we live in separate houses," Gabrielli would say to her, when she urged them to reconsider their resolution to live apart. "Your husband, and your father, and myself, will be fast friends, if we only meet every day, to talk about you, and to dispute each other's opinions on all other matters. We shall quarrel most agreeably, I assure you, as long as we know that we are not forced to come together against our inclinations."

"But what should you quarrel about at all?" replied Francesca.

"Ah! *carina*," he answered, "you have no idea how the instinct of pugnacity will develop in me, now that I am a lonely old man no more. I shall quarrel with your husband about sculpture, and with your father about politics, and we shall all love each other the more for it."

"Be satisfied, child," interposed her father. "He is in the right."

And thus it came to pass that to this day there is no brighter a houschold in Rome than that of which the mosaic-worker's daughter is the life and soul. The ideal head of Italy, sadly dreaming over her long-lost liberties, is still unfinished, for D'Urbino protests that Francesca's countenance now never wears that look of indescribable and passionate sadness, which first began to awaken him to the sweetness and the nobility of a character, which, till he had learned to know her, he had thought impossible in women.

THE END.

BILLING, PRINTER, GUILDFORD.

www.ingramcontent.com/pod-product-compliance
Lightning Source LLC
Chambersburg PA
CBHW021959220426
43663CB00007B/875